Your Guide to a Joyful, Stress-Free Life

FIND YOUR CALM

What, Why and How
MEDITATION

SP SINGH

BLUEROSE PUBLISHERS
India | U.K.

Copyright © SP Singh 2025

All rights reserved by author. No part of this publication may be reproduced, stored in a retrieval system or transmitted in any form or by any means, electronic, mechanical, photocopying, recording or otherwise, without the prior permission of the author. Although every precaution has been taken to verify the accuracy of the information contained herein, the publisher assumes no responsibility for any errors or omissions. No liability is assumed for damages that may result from the use of information contained within.

BlueRose Publishers takes no responsibility for any damages, losses, or liabilities that may arise from the use or misuse of the information, products, or services provided in this publication.

For permissions requests or inquiries regarding this publication, please contact:

BLUEROSE PUBLISHERS
www.BlueRoseONE.com
info@bluerosepublishers.com
+91 8882 898 898
+4407342408967

ISBN: 978-93-6783-389-6

Cover Design: Shubham
Typesetting: Sagar

First Edition: January 2025

Disclaimer

This book integrates insights from the latest scientific developments in yoga and meditation, the wisdom of ancient scriptures, and the author's deep understanding and extensive practice in yoga. The author has meticulously worked to ensure the information is accurate, comprehensive, and presented in a manner accessible to readers from all walks of life.

The information in this book is intended to provide readers with a better understanding of meditation. However, the author does not claim the authenticity of the facts, and readers are advised to use their discretion when following any practices or recommendations described in this book. The author assumes no responsibility for errors, omissions, or consequences of using this information.

This book is intended for informational purposes and is not a substitute for professional medical advice, diagnosis, or treatment. Readers should always consult their healthcare provider before starting any new exercise or health regimen. The author is not liable for any damages or losses that may arise from the use of this information

Preface

Imagine if I were to tell you about a simple daily practice that could help alleviate stress and anxiety, increase your focus and willpower, and even boost your emotional intelligence, memory, and intuition.

Would you be interested in learning about it?

What if I also told you that this practice has no harmful side effects?

It's all-natural and will cost you nothing. Would you like to know more about it?

Well, that practice is meditation. By activating our body's inner pharmacy, meditation can profoundly impact our mental, emotional, and physical well-being. So, if you're looking for a natural and accessible way to improve your life, why not try meditation?

Meditation, as a practice, transcends specific regions or cultures and has been embraced in various forms worldwide for centuries. In recent decades, the Western world and other areas have shown an increasing interest in Indian meditation practices, owing to India's profound history of meditation with a tradition spanning millennia.

India is renowned as the birthplace of diverse meditation techniques, including Yoga and Vipassana, which have gained popularity in the West. In our fast-paced, stress-laden contemporary society, people are increasingly seeking effective means to manage stress, enhance their mental well-being, and attain inner tranquility. Meditation is widely recognized as a valuable tool for achieving these objectives. Moreover, recent years have witnessed a growing body of scientific research that underscores meditation's mental and physical health benefits.

Having attended many schools, met many teachers, and read many books, I have come to understand meditation. It has immensely helped me manage my personal and professional life. In my personal experience, no other practice can benefit us physically, mentally, intellectually, and spiritually to the extent meditation can.

The best practice is to have a good theory. We need to understand something before we practice it to make it part of our lives or reap the complete benefits. So, understanding something before we practice it is part of practice.

This book aims to provide a basic understanding of meditation, including what it is, why it is important, how to do it, and its benefits in the minimum amount of time possible.

I understand that we need to practice or learn from others' experiences to make them our own experiences.

With practice, readers will get a taste of meditation.

This book can serve as a helpful guide to beginners looking to start their meditation journey. This book will also help those who have some meditation experience and want to deepen their understanding.

I want to express my gratitude to all the mystics and teachers who have shared their experiences and understanding of meditation for the benefit of humanity. Their efforts have made it possible for us to understand meditation in theory before practicing it; otherwise, it would have been a tedious journey.

I would also like to thank my wife, Sanjana, for her support and inspiration in writing this book. I thank one and all.

While writing this book, I structured it as a discourse to aid in better understanding.

I understand that what I share in this book has already been said by mystics and shared by different people in different ways. However, I see myself as a medium who has spent much time understanding meditation and bringing it together concisely as per my understanding and knowledge. This book will help inspire readers to practice meditation and immensely benefit their lives. I struggled a lot to understand meditation, and I hope you do not need to go through all that. This book will ease your journey.

I respectfully urge you to embark on your meditation journey, immerse yourself in the experience, and motivate your dear ones to live a life of well-being and joy.

I wish all the readers a happy, healthy, and meditative Life."

Introduction

"Have you ever felt overwhelmed by your thoughts and emotions?"

"Are you looking for a way to reduce stress and improve your well-being?". If you answer yes, you are at the right place doing the right thing.

Namaste and welcome. Congratulations on your decision to choose this book.

Before we start, let me quote Swami Vivekananda on the nature of the mind and the need for meditation. Swami Vivekananda said, 'How hard it is to control the mind! Has it been compared to a maddened monkey who is drunk and stung by a scorpion, and a demon also entered him? The human mind is like that monkey, restless.'

He also said, "The first lesson is to sit for some time and let the mind run on. Until you know what your mind is doing, you cannot control it. In the first few months, you will find that the mind will have many thoughts. Later, you will find that they have somewhat decreased, and in a few more months, they will be fewer and fewer until last, the mind will be under perfect control, but we must patiently practice every day."

"The Meditation must begin with gross objects and slowly rise to finer and finer until it becomes objectless. The mind should first receive the external causes of sensation, then the internal motions, and then its reaction".

He further said, "It is easy to concentrate the mind on external things; the mind naturally goes outwards, but not so in the case of religion, psychology, or metaphysics where the subject and the object are one. The object is internal, the mind itself is the object, and it is necessary to study the mind itself- mind studying the mind."

"Practice is necessary. You may sit down and listen to me for hours daily, but you will only get one step further if you practice. It all depends on practice. We never understand these things unless we experience them. We will have to see and feel them for ourselves. Simply listening to explanations and theories will not do."

The words of Swami Vivekananda provide a clear understanding and framework for meditation.

In this book, we will learn and acquire sufficient knowledge of meditation, its benefits, as per the latest scientific findings, and how to meditate.

For a better understanding, we will divide our study of meditation into five parts. Part I will focus on why we need meditation. Part II will cover what meditation is, while Part III will focus on the how of meditation. In Part IV, we will explore the benefits of meditation according to the latest scientific findings. Finally, in Part V, we will learn about Meditation practice through some guided meditation.

Furthermore, each part consists of five to six chapters. The entire book has been designed to be concise, allowing readers to complete all parts efficiently and incorporate meditation as a daily practice, thereby benefiting from it.

Blaise Pascal once said, "All men's miseries derive from not being able to sit in a quiet room alone."

This book aims to help us sit alone and realize that we are complete and the source of all bliss lies within us. However, understanding alone is not enough; we must experience it like love. We can truly understand love once we experience it; the same is true for meditation.

The more important work we do as part of our livelihood, the more important it becomes to take better care of ourselves, and meditation is the ultimate practice that helps us to do this.

No one will take care of us unless we start taking care of ourselves, and meditation is the method.

Meditation is not just a spiritual practice reserved for those seeking enlightenment. It has become a trendy, mainstream activity that can help us transform our body, mind, and approach to life.

Meditation is about noticing something that we did not notice before. We often live like robots, with 90% of our thoughts being the same as yesterday, and we repeat the same habits and routines. We must become aware of this to make any lasting changes.

Our relationship with ourselves predicts our relationship with the world. Through meditation, in solitude, we receive insights that transform us. Immersing ourselves in stillness and silence helps us discover who we are. Ultimately, we are the only person who will be with us our entire life. Why not strengthen our relationship with ourselves and start a lifetime love affair? Meditation is the way to enhance this relationship and enjoy our own company.

Meditation involves all aspects of our lives and can be a solution to all the problems of life.

All methods of meditation involve unconditioning. Ideology or moral education alone cannot alter our genetic impressions and biological cells. A deep understanding and scientific approach, combined with regular practice, are necessary to bring about changes from the inside out.

I invite you to continue on this journey, to learn and practice meditation regularly, and to start a lifetime love affair with yourself. Thank you for choosing this book, and best of luck in your meditation journey.

Keep meditating!

Contents

Disclaimer iii
Preface iv
Introduction vii

Part I: Why Meditation 1

Chapter-1: Why Meditation: Statistics 2

Chapter-2: Why Meditation- Most efficient way to deal
Imagined Stress & Negative Emotions. 6

Chapter-3: Why Meditation- Excellent Exercise for the Brain 10

Chapter-4: Why Meditation- Ultimate source of Happiness. 14

Chapter-5: Why Meditation- The technique to Rewrite
the Genetic Code. 18

Chapter-6: Why Meditation- The secret to Mastering Emotion. 21

Part II: What Is Meditation 27

Chapter-1: Meditation- The optimum utilization of the
Human Brain - The Neocortex. 28

Chapter-2: Meditation- "Chitta vritti nirodha- The cessation
of thought and state of relaxation. 32

Chapter-3: Meditation- Technique to come out of the grip of the past,
instinctive brain, ego and fear of death. 35

Chapter-4: Meditation- Beyond Thinking, Contemplation, Concentration. 40

Chapter-5: Meditation: Observation and witnessing without identification. 43

Chapter-6: Meditation is self-remembrance 47

Chapter-7: Meditation: The awareness of separateness from
the state of waking, sleeping and dreaming. 51

Chapter-8: Meditation: Tool to purify our mind & surrender
our ego to our higher self. 55

Part III: How Meditation 59

Chapter-1: How Meditation: No suppression of
thoughts but persuasion. 60

Chapter-2: How Meditation: The single pointed focus
on sense objects from gross to subtle. 63

Chapter-3: How Meditation: The observation of breath-
Bridge between body & Mind. 68

Chapter-4: How Meditation: Controlling the Movement of Eyes:
The widow to the Brain. 74

Chapter-5: How Meditation: The observation of mind i.e.
the process of thinking. 77

Part IV: Benefits of Meditation 81

Chapter-1: Meditation Strengthen key brain region : Harness the power of
meditation to make your brain smarter, happier & healthier. 82

Chapter-2: Meditation Develops Prefrontal Cortex 93

Chapter-3: Meditation helps in: Longevity,
Life Extension, & Anti-Aging. 99

Chapter-4: Meditation Helps: Lose Weight, Achieve Ideal Body 106

Chapter 5: Meditation, Naturally Boosts Good Brain Chemicals 110

Chapter-6: Meditation: Boost Immunity, Build Health, Beat Disease. 115

Part V: Meditation Practice 119

Chater-1: Meditation Practice 120

Biblography: Resources 137

Part I:
Why Meditation

Chapter-I

Why Meditation: Statistics

Greetings and welcome to the first chapter of our discussion on Why meditation through enlightening statistics. Meditation, an age-old practice, is experiencing a modern resurgence, offering a path to inner peace and well-being that is more relevant than ever. In today's discussion, we will explore the remarkable rise in the popularity of meditation through some statistics, revealing how it has become an integral part of countless lives worldwide.

Globally, an estimated 300 to 500 million individuals have embraced meditation as an essential component of their lives. This vast and diverse community transcends cultural boundaries, demonstrating the universal appeal of meditation in the pursuit of well-being.

Surveys indicate that in 2012, merely 4.1% of U.S. adults reported using meditation over the course of a year, and in 2017, that number significantly increased to 14%, signifying a growing recognition of the practice's benefits in coping with the stresses of contemporary life.

One of the most intriguing statistics uncovered is that 70% of meditation practitioners have been engaging in this practice for less than two years.

This suggests that many individuals embrace meditation as a relatively new addition to their lives, highlighting its accessibility and adaptability.

When it comes to the frequency of practice, the average person meditates 2-3 days per week. While 51% meditate three days per week or less, 16% have made it a daily practice. The majority, however, have found their equilibrium by meditating three days a week, showcasing the flexibility of this practice. Surprisingly, 88% of meditators allocate 30 minutes or less to their meditation sessions. With 41% meditating for 15 minutes or less and 47% dedicating 15-30 minutes, it's evident that meditation can seamlessly integrate into even the busiest daily routines.

Why do people turn to meditation? As per statistics, an overwhelming 84% cite stress and anxiety reduction as their primary motivation. However, the benefits extend far beyond stress relief, with practitioners seeking improved concentration and memory (53%), enhanced performance at work or school (52%), increased energy (39%), general health and wellness (30%), improved attitude and outlook on life (28%), and even spiritual growth (21%). These statistics reveal that people are drawn to meditation for its multifaceted advantages.

The journey of meditation is often personal, with 87% of practitioners choosing to meditate alone. However, meditation's adaptability shines through in the 13% who prefer group meditation, blending community benefits with inner reflection.

As we consider those who have yet to embrace meditation, it's important to note that 33% cite a lack of knowledge as the primary reason for not meditating, indicating an opportunity for education and awareness. Furthermore, 27% mention time constraints, and 25% express skepticism about its benefits

This book will help to bridge these gaps, offering readers knowledge and guidance, sharing scientifically proven benefits of meditation, and providing support for making meditation an integral part of busy daily life.

Further, the research conducted by Tim Ferris, the author of the book "4 Hour Work Week," revealed that almost 90% of successful CEOs, Hollywood actors, bestselling authors, bloggers, media personalities, military leaders, artists, and Olympic athletes practice meditation daily.

Meditation is not just a practice for spiritual gurus or monks secluded in mountain retreats; it's a powerful tool embraced by numerous famous personalities from diverse fields who have integrated it into their busy lives. Many superachievers and billionaires attribute their success to meditation. Microsoft co-founder Bill Gates has often cited meditation as a powerful tool for improving his focus and decision-making abilities. Jeff Weiner, Executive Chairman of LinkedIn; William Clay Ford Jr., Executive Chairman of Ford Motor Company; Salesforce CEO Marc Benioff , also attribute their success to meditation.

The late Steve Jobs, the visionary behind Apple Company, was known for his meditation practice. Legendary billionaire investor Ray Dalio has stated that meditation is the most crucial reason for his incredible track record of success.

However, meditation is not reserved for the elite or the business world. It's a practice embraced by many famous personalities from diverse fields. By dedicating even a few minutes a day to this practice, we can tap into a wellspring of inner peace and clarity. It's a simple yet potent means to enhance focus, reduce stress, and embark on a journey towards a more balanced and fulfilling life.

Many corporate companies, like Google, Apple, P&G, IBM, and Nike, have recognized the immense value of offering meditation and mindfulness programs to their employees. During my stay in Hyderabad City in the south of India, I, too, had the opportunity to teach yoga/meditation to employees of Microsoft, Google, GE, Capgemini, Reliance JP Morgan, etc. These initiatives aim to promote mental and emotional well-being among staff members, reduce workplace stress, and enhance overall productivity.

By providing access to meditation resources and mindfulness training, these companies are equipping their workforce with tools to navigate the demands of the modern workplace more effectively. Such programs also contribute to a positive company culture, fostering a more relaxed and balanced environment where employees can thrive both personally and professionally.

Today, our brains are bombarded with more information than ever before. With the rise of mobile devices, the Internet, laptops, computers, and television, we are constantly exposed to the outside world.

Most of our jobs involve heavy use of the brain, overburdening the mind. This sedentary lifestyle and increased stress are leading to a rise in psychosomatic diseases that affect both mind and body.

Despite advances in science and technology, the modern world is struggling to address the increase in stress, anxiety, and psychosomatic diseases. Modern medicine focuses on treating the body from the outside but cannot reach a person's innermost being. Psychosomatic diseases begin in the mind and can only be cured from within.

The mind and body are interconnected; when the mind is disturbed, it can manifest as physical ailments. Meditation is the only way to heal the mind and body from within. There are more than 100 meditation techniques, each aimed at using the mind differently.

Meditation is a medicine for the mind, and it has become a way of life for millions of people seeking inner peace and well-being.

In our upcoming discussions, we will explore meditation in greater detail; remember to keep meditating.

CHAPTER-2

Why Meditation- Most efficient way to deal Imagined Stress & Negative Emotions.

Namaste, welcome to the second chapter of our discussion on why Meditation. Today, we will explore the role of Meditation in dealing with imagined stress and negative emotions. Acute stress is the most common type of stress, often triggered by thinking about past pressures or future demands.

Did you know that research shows that imagining a threat can trigger the same regions in our brain as actually experiencing it? Our brain doesn't distinguish between real and imaginary threats, and the stress response is activated regardless.

This response is designed to prepare us for danger but imagined threats can also trigger it. These trigger the release of cortisol and adrenaline and affect our immune system and overall health.

The stress response evolved in humans to allow us to fight or flee when faced with danger. Chemicals, including cortisol and adrenaline, help kick-start the body, pushing blood towards the major muscles and helping us face the challenge. But the same stress response kicks in when we imagine danger, also producing cortisol and adrenaline and pushing blood around the body. The same chemistry is produced regardless of whether the threat is real or imagined.

What does all this mean in real life? It means that what we imagine is happening as far as our brain is concerned, and our body responds accordingly. This causes the release and accumulation of cortisol/adrenaline, affecting our immune system and overall health. Our bodies do not know the difference between real-life and imagined experiences; they behave similarly.

A famous experiment conducted by Abu Ali Sina, the father of early modern medicine, involved putting two identical lambs in separate cages. He placed a wolf in one of the cages, which could only be seen by one of the lambs. Months later, the lamb that had seen the wolf died out of fear and stress, even though the wolf had not harmed it. The other lamb that had not seen the wolf remained healthy. This experiment shows how unnecessary fear and stress can damage and even kill us.

Humans also face many "wolves" daily, such as demanding bosses, irritating colleagues, traffic jams, etc.

According to an article published by the National Science Foundation in 2005, the average person has between 12,000 and 60,000 thoughts daily. Of those, 80% are harmful, and 95% are repetitive thoughts from the previous day. Our thoughts and feelings directly affect our bodies, and our thoughts shape our destiny.

It's no surprise that life can be miserable if we don't know how to master our minds. We have so many negative thoughts every day, and our brains cannot distinguish between real and imagined threats.

By age 35, 95% of our thoughts are unconscious, and 70% are survival-related. An interesting example of the mind-body connection is the fear response in lambs. Even if a wolf is in a cage, the constant fear and anxiety can lead to the lamb's death.

Similarly, we are often in a constant state of fear and anxiety due to stressors in our daily lives. This happens without our knowledge because our subconscious mind, which controls bodily functions like heartbeat, circulation, and respiration, cannot differentiate between actual experiences and thoughts.

Every time we have negative thoughts or emotions like fear, anger, hatred, or stress, our body reacts as if they are real. Even anticipating a stressful situation can cause changes in our blood pressure, heart rate, breathing pattern, and chemical balance as if we are experiencing stress. Unsurprisingly, many of the problems modern humans face are related to the mind.

Imagine you are in a cab heading to the airport to catch a flight for an important job interview in another city. You left home on time, confident about reaching the airport. However, halfway through the journey, you encounter a massive traffic jam caused by an accident.

At that moment, most of us instinctively begin imagining the worst-case scenario: missing the flight, failing to attend the interview, and losing the job opportunity. The traffic is clearing very slowly, yet these negative thoughts keep recurring. Whenever you think about missing the flight, your mind behaves like the worst has already happened.

This triggers your body's stress response. Your heart rate increases, your blood pressure rises, and your body releases cortisol, the stress hormone. This happens repeatedly as you stay caught in a loop of negative anticipation. Whether or not you ultimately miss the flight, your body and mind react as if the worst has already occurred, causing significant mental and physical strain.

We encounter such situations every day in different ways—imagining not meeting deadlines, failing exams, not getting a job, or not finding a suitable marriage match. The list goes on. Imagined stress affects all of us, often without awareness, as our thoughts create real physiological and emotional consequences before anything happens.

It is rightly said that the heaviest burdens we carry are the thoughts in our head, and the heavier our cart becomes, the more we hold on. As per the statistics, 75% to 90% of all doctor's office visits in the USA are for stress-related diseases and complaints; the situation may be the same all over the world. If not today or tomorrow, it may happen. It is time to do something about mind-oriented diseases; otherwise, we will never be able to eradicate all body-oriented diseases.

Chronic stress is linked to six leading causes of death, including heart disease, lung ailments, cancer, accidents, cirrhosis of the liver, and suicide, according to the American Psychological Association. Stress is a leading cause of premature deaths and can also be linked to causes of death due to dementia and diabetes.

Meditation can help us become aware of our thoughts and emotions. In this awareness, we can recognize that what we imagine is just an imagination, and our brain and body are not affected as they are when we are unaware. Understanding that every negative thought drains our energy and harms us makes us alert, and we start avoiding such thoughts. Instead, we can induce thoughts of gratitude, hope, forgiveness, kindness, trust, empathy, etc.

Whatever we spend our time mentally attending to is what we are and will become. So, why not be aware and eliminate negative thoughts?

This understanding will help you continue your meditation journey and reduce stress.

Chapter-3

Why Meditation- Excellent Exercise for the Brain

Namaste, welcome to our discussion on the Why of Meditation, Chapter 3. Today, we will explore how Meditation is an excellent exercise for the brain.

Our body and mind are interconnected. We are body-mind, which means the body is the external mind and the mind is the internal body; there is no division. Our thoughts can affect our feelings, and vice versa.

Persistent worries and stress can lead to tense muscles, pain, headaches, and stomach problems, as well as more serious issues like high blood pressure. Statistics from the National Headache Foundation in America reveal that 45 million Americans suffer from headaches, with 90% of them being caused by stress, anxiety, and tension.

The mind-body connection is so strong that even the slightest feeling of fear, depression, nervousness, or anxiety can manifest in our body language.

Similarly, pain or a headache can make us worried or mentally disturbed.

The physiological process and mental processes are two parts of one mechanism.

Whatever we do physiologically affects the mind, and whatever we do psychologically affects the body.

Each emotion and psychological aspect of our being has a physiological basis somewhere deep down. Just as our muscles require exercise to grow stronger, our memory, willpower, creativity, and other psychological aspects also have a physiological basis that can be improved through Meditation.

Meditation is the mental gym for our brain. It's a path to elevating our cognitive capabilities. As exercise strengthens our muscles and enhances our physical abilities, Meditation acts as an exercise for the brain, leading to improved cognitive functions. Our brain is intricately connected to our psychological well-being, and different mental abilities are associated with specific brain regions.

As per the scientific findings our brain develops through neural connections. Neurons, the information processing cells in our brain, connect to make neural pathways, which are responsible for our thoughts, sensations, feelings and actions.

When we repeatedly engage in an activity like Meditation, we strengthen the neural connections involved. This develops the different regions of our brain and, in turn, our mental abilities.

By working with our physiological base, i.e., the physical part of the brain, through Meditation, we can positively influence our mental aspects. Meditation improves our mental well-being as a result as it's an exercise for the brain.

Memory, for example, is known to have roots in the hippocampus, a physiological part of the brain. By working with our physiological base, we can positively influence our psychological aspects, and this is precisely what Meditation does. Meditation improves our psychological well-being as a result.

One example is that Meditation reduces stress responses and ends anxiety by reducing the size of the amygdala, the primitive "fear center" in our brain, which helps in avoiding amygdala hijack. Through our senses, we perceive and identify stressors, and the amygdala, the part of the brain primarily involved in emotion, memory, and fight-or-flight responses, responds by initiating the body's coping mechanisms to deal with the perceived threat. The hypothalamus then communicates with the pituitary gland, which releases hormones that signal the adrenal gland to release corresponding hormones, such as adrenaline, nor-adrenaline, and epinephrine, to prepare the body for fight or flight.

These hormones facilitate the immediate physical reactions associated with the preparation for muscular action, such as acceleration of the heart to pump more blood to the extremities, acceleration of the lungs to pump more oxygen and glucose, slowing of digestion to redirect energy for immediate use, constriction of blood vessels to carry blood to the extremities quickly, liberation of metabolic energy sources (i.e., fat and glycogen) for muscular energy, dilation of pupils to improve focus, loss of peripheral vision to improve focus, and increased muscle tension for running or fighting. The sympathetic nervous system manages these physiological changes by increasing heart rate, blood pressure, and insulin levels.

However, modern-day stressors are typically psychological, and the sympathetic nervous system often remains overactive, while the parasympathetic nervous system rarely gets a chance to play its role. Meditation can help us reduce the size of the amygdala, which in turn reduces stress responses and ends anxiety.

Meditation can also help us activate the parasympathetic nervous system, which allows us relax and unwind. During Meditation, the body's relaxation response is triggered, which reduces heart rate, blood pressure, and muscle tension while increasing alpha brainwave activity. As a result, the parasympathetic nervous system is activated, and the body can enter a state of deep relaxation. With regular meditation, the body can learn to cope with stress more efficiently by activating the relaxation response more readily, improving overall well-being.

In 2011, researchers from the Massachusetts General Hospital conducted fMRI brain scans of 51 adults before and after eight weeks of mindful meditation training. The meditators were found to have effectively silenced the electrical activity within their primitive amygdala, resulting in fewer anxiety, worry, and fear signals in their brains. What's more, these participants had significantly decreased the size/volume of their amygdala in less than two months, which was a groundbreaking discovery.

For a more detailed understanding of the different physiological parts of the brain, their connection with psychological aspects, and the role of Meditation in improving relationships, increasing feelings of well-being, and enhancing creativity, intuition, and willpower, please refer to the benefits of Meditation in part IV of this book. There are numerous benefits of Meditation and I feel one book is not enough to enumerate the same. . Please do your own research as well.

I hope this discussion has inspired you to continue on your meditation journey.

Keep meditating!

Chapter-4

Why Meditation- Ultimate source of Happiness.

Welcome to the discussion on why meditation, Chapter 4.

Today, we will explore how meditation can help us achieve the state of ultimate joy and bliss.

We will understand how meditation is a real source of happiness.

Humans always pursue happiness, and avoiding pain and seeking pleasure is natural. However, what is the secret to achieving true and lasting happiness? Happiness varies from person to person, and what makes one person happy may not have the same effect on someone else due to differences in personal preferences, belief systems, and upbringing.

Therefore, happiness is subjective and varies from individual to individual.

The concept of Hedonic Adaptation, also known as the "hedonic treadmill," suggests that while good events may bring happiness at the moment, happiness is often short-lived.

As humans, we tend to look for new experiences and stimuli to maintain our happiness, often becoming desensitized to the things that once brought us joy. This treadmill effect can lead to a never-ending cycle of wanting more and feeling unsatisfied, making it challenging to maintain lasting happiness.

Furthermore, the Law of Diminishing Returns applies to pursuing a sense of pleasure. Overindulgence in repetitive or excessive sensory experiences can decrease enjoyment and disgust.

Imagine taking a bite of your favorite chocolate and feeling the joy it brings. But as we continue to eat more chocolates, the pleasure we initially experienced fades away, and the level of satisfaction decreases with each repetition. Hence, gratifying our senses alone cannot be the secret to happiness.

If we analyze happiness more deeply, we realize that being engaged in an intellectual pursuit and experiencing a state of concentration, free from distractions, such as writing a novel, reading a book, playing chess, or working on a science project, can bring us closer to a state of happiness.

However, it is essential to note that overexerting mental energy for prolonged periods can lead to strain and fatigue. Therefore, while concentration is necessary, it alone cannot guarantee the secret to happiness.

Sometimes, we seek happiness through adventurous activities, but a prolonged thrill period does not always lead to increased happiness. Instead, it can weaken our senses, leaving us exhausted in the end.

Therefore, it is essential to balance gratifying our senses, engaging in intellectual pursuits, and pursuing adventures to achieve happiness.

But what to do for enteral happiness? What is the secret to eternal joy and happiness?

According to the Upanishads' analysis of happiness, when we seek happiness by gratifying our senses and seeking pleasure outside of ourselves, we become so engrossed in the activity that we lose touch with reality and only grasp the superficial like the swirling of a lighted stick giving the impression of a circle of light. We assume that happiness comes from the gratification of our senses, but in reality, it is a false impression because if it were true, our happiness would have increased, but it does not.

If we observe more deeply, we find that whenever we are involved in any sense of pleasure, it is not the involvement of the sense that brings joy but rather the silence of the mind. For example, when we take the first bite of our favorite chocolate, our sense of taste becomes so dominant that all other thoughts vanish, distractions cease, and we experience a moment of bliss. However, this state only lasts for a fraction of a second.

The actual reason behind joy is the mind in a non-thinking phase, or a state of no mind, not the taste. Similarly, the sense of vision can also bring us to a state of joy when we witness the beauty of the Himalayas or watch the sunset on a beach.

To truly understand the secret of joy and happiness, we must look beyond the mere sense of gratification and distractions. While it is natural for humans to seek pleasure and avoid pain, the trustworthy source of joy lies in silencing the mind and reaching a state of no distraction.

Sense enjoyment, such as watching a movie, can provide temporary joy. Still, as the law of diminishing returns kicks in, it becomes harder to find the same level of pleasure in repeating the same activity.

The most calm and peaceful state is when the five senses and mind are settled down in a state of no distraction. Meditation can achieve this state, which is a state of no mind, no distraction, and no thought.

However, since our sense organs and mind are constantly in contact with the world around us, it can be challenging to maintain this state of peace and tranquility in our daily lives. Nevertheless, meditation provides a way out of the cycle of seeking joy through temporary sense pleasures, and instead, allows us to tap into the eternal source of happiness that lies within us.

In meditation, the law of diminishing returns, or hedonic adaptation, does not apply. On the contrary, as we become consistent with our practice, achieving a state of salience becomes more manageable, and it takes less and less time to reach a state of no mind. This results in a state of bliss where we are not just experiencing bliss but are also one with it.

Meditation is a scientific way to realize our actual state, which is the state of ultimate bliss - "Sachchidanand" or "Sat chit Anand " (truth, consciousness, bliss). This state is achieved by increasing alpha wave activity in the brain during meditation. Alpha waves are neural oscillations in the brain's thalamic pacemaker cells in the 8-12 Hz frequency range, which can be detected by EEG (electroencephalogram). Unlike drowsiness, the relaxed state indicated by alpha waves is quite alert, and it drives the power of now.

Permanent happiness cannot be achieved by consuming something or, going somewhere or doing something. Why spend billions of rupees searching for happiness elsewhere when we can find it right here and right now through meditation?

Harvard psychologists Matthew A. Killingsworth and Daniel T. Gilbert researched wandering minds using a "track your happiness" iPhone app. The findings show that people spend 46.9% of their waking hours thinking about something other than what they are doing, and this mind-wandering typically makes them unhappy. Therefore, the research concludes that a wandering mind is an unhappy mind.

So, to achieve true happiness, it is essential to slow down the speed of the mind or enter a state of no reason, which is a blissful state of being. This is where there are no thoughts, and we experience true happiness. Meditation can help us achieve this state of no mind and bring us closer to ultimate bliss.

This understanding will help you continue your meditation journey.

Remember to keep meditating and experience ultimate joy and bliss.

Chapter-5

Why Meditation- The technique to Rewrite the Genetic Code.

Greetings, and welcome to Chapter 5 of the Why of Meditation discussion series. Today, we will delve into how our genes influence our personality traits and how meditation can help us break free from the limitations of our genetic code, allowing us to shape our future.

Have you ever pondered upon the reasons behind our current state of being? Have you thought about how we became the way we are and what it takes to transform ourselves through the power of intentional thoughts and meditation?

Genetics plays a significant role, with researchers estimating that up to 50% of our personality traits are inherited from our parents. We learn and internalize their thought patterns, feelings, and experiences, which shape the foundation of our being. However, we also have the power to modify what we've inherited and create new neurological capital.

We inherit our parents' knowledge, thought patterns, and emotions, which lay the foundation for who we become. Our learned memories from previous generations also serve as a foundation for creating new memories.

However, we may have inherited genetic codes for negative traits such as anger, victimization, insecurity, and low self-esteem.

If these cells continue to fire together, they develop stronger connections, making us more prone to these negative traits and victims of our genetic makeup.

With the emergence of the science of epigenetics, which studies how our behaviors and environment can cause changes that affect how our genes work, we are no longer victims of our genetics. The idea that genes are "set in stone" or that genes alone determine our development has been disproven.

The nature versus nurture debate is no longer relevant, as it is now understood that nature and nurture play a crucial role in shaping who we are.

To evolve ourselves, we must learn to add and modify what we have been initially given. Our environment, or nurture, plays a crucial role in shaping us. Every time we learn something new, our sense of self is altered. Our genetic inheritance serves as only the initial deposit of our neurological capital, and it is not the end-all-be-all of who we are.

If we repeatedly fire the same genetically inherited circuits of corresponding emotions, we wire ourselves to live our predetermined genetic destiny. Similarly, if we repeat the same familiar routines, automatic actions, habits, and behaviors, our brains will remain the same, and we will stagnate.

As long as we consciously become aware of our genetics, we can break free from our unconscious patterns of living and avoid being a victim of them. Meditation can be the way out. Neuroplasticity is the brain's ability to change and adapt, and it is possible to rewire our brains by repeatedly activating new neural connections through meditation.

Neuroplasticity gives our brains the ability to change. The adult brain continues to grow and change throughout our lives, and what we learn and how we remember shapes who we are. To escape our genetic inheritance, it is essential to become aware of our unconscious thoughts and robot-like habits. Continuously learning new information and having new experiences is a way out, and meditation can help us achieve this.

Through meditation, we learn to be aware and not robot-like. With this awareness, we can learn new habits, and with repeated activation of new neural connections, they slowly become hardwired. Old patterns are pruned away, and we become new beings.

As Einstein said, no problem can be solved with the same level of consciousness that created it. Meditation takes us to a higher level of our existence, and it is an effective tool for breaking free from our genetic inheritance and living the life of our dreams.

Meditation is how to become conscious, attentive, aware, and present. When truly mindful, we change how the brain works to create a new level of mind. In meditation, the brain circuits associated with time, space, and sensory perception quiet down.

One becomes utterly detached from one's body and environment, and even the concept of time disappears. Meditation provides an opportunity to detach from the past and create a new possibility for the future.

Once the physical body has been trained to know what the mind knows, that vital information is passed on to the next generation; by neurologically encoding repeated events through the mastery of learning and experience, we will genetically become what we have mastered. Meditation helps us create new genes and an evolved generation.

So meditation provides a way to break free from our genetic destiny and create a new future by changing our brains and genetic makeup.

This understanding will help you continue your journey of meditation.

Keep meditating!

Chapter-6

Why Meditation-
The secret to Mastering Emotion.

Namaste, welcome to the series of discussions on Why of Meditation Chapter 6. In this chapter, we will discuss how our thoughts and emotions shape our reality and how meditation can help us become more conscious of them and create the life of our dreams.

We cannot change what we are not aware of. To create a new reality, we must become aware of our unconscious thoughts, automatic behavior, and emotional reactions that we have been conditioned to. Meditation is a powerful tool that helps us become conscious of these programs and initiate change.

Buddha once said, "All that we are is the result of what we have thought." Our minds are incredibly powerful, but we rarely analyze how we think. Our thoughts are like seeds; what we think directly influences how we feel and behave.

Our thoughts have a profound impact on our emotions and actions. If we constantly think negatively about ourselves, we will start to feel negative emotions and act in negative ways that reinforce our beliefs about ourselves.

For example, if we believe we are a failure, we will feel like a failure and act in ways that confirm this belief. We may view every mistake as proof that we are not good enough and attribute our successes to luck rather than our abilities.

In this way, our thoughts shape our feelings, actions, and ultimately our reality. It is important to become aware of these patterns and learn to challenge and reframe our negative thoughts to create a more positive and empowering mindset.

The good news is that we can change how we think and alter our perceptions, leading to a more optimistic outlook on life. By letting go of self-limiting beliefs, we can reach our full potential and engage in productive behavior, increasing our chances of success.

Meditation is a powerful tool that can help us achieve this. One of Buddha's most important teachings is that our past does not solely determine our present experiences. While some of our experiences may be influenced by our past, it is ultimately our present intentions that shape how we perceive and respond to the world around us. Meditation can help us cultivate present-moment awareness and mindfulness, allowing us to better manage our thoughts and emotions and choose how we respond to the world.

As per modern psychology, there are three main theories of emotions formulated by groups of different psychologists: 1) the James-Lange Theory, 2) the Cannon-Bard Theory, and 3) the Cognitive Theory or Two-Factor Theory (Stanley Schachter and Jerome Singer). Out of these, the Two-Factor Theory is widely accepted.

According to the Two-Factor Theory of Emotion, the arousal we experience is basically the same in every emotion, and all feelings are differentiated only by our cognitive appraisal of the source of the arousal. This theory asserts that the experience of emotion is determined by the intensity of the arousal we are experiencing, but the cognitive appraisal of the situation determines what the emotion will be.

Modern psychologists have found and proved that we are more influenced by our perception of how we should be feeling (our cognition) than by how we feel (arousal).

Meditation helps us become aware of our cognition. With practice, we can train our brains to think differently, enabling us to master our minds and emotions.

Emotions result from our repetitive thought patterns. If we consistently experience certain emotions over a long period, they become our mood, which eventually shapes our temperament and personality. This means that our thoughts have a significant impact on our reality, as our thoughts become our personalities.

Our brain forms long-term memories with intense emotional experiences. When we pay attention to negative emotions, we are giving them more energy, and our body becomes conditioned to crave those emotions. This can lead to a vicious cycle of negative thinking and emotions, where we start accessing those negative emotions even when we are not experiencing them in our day-to-day lives.

Meditation is a powerful tool for breaking this cycle. Meditative practices help raise our awareness to a measurable higher state, which in turn reduces the volume of negative thoughts and emotions. With regular meditation practice, we can maintain this higher state of awareness. There is no need to fight with individual emotions, as raising consciousness through meditation can take care of all negative emotions.

It's like lighting a lamp in a dark room, and all the darkness disappears, no matter how dark the room is or how long it has been dark.

To make an immediate change in our thought patterns, we need to become conscious of our thought processes and actions. Meditation helps us become aware of our thoughts and actions, allowing us to break the cycle of negative thinking and create a more positive outlook. By changing our present, we can change our future and become the creators of our own life.

With regular meditation practice, we can become the master of our own emotions, and the people around us no longer have control over our emotional state. We are in control of our own lives and can create a positive and fulfilling reality for ourselves.

Meditation brings about numerous physiological changes in the frontal lobes, also known as the neocortex, which is a gift of evolution to us. The neocortex is responsible for planning, imagination, control, and regulation of other parts of the brain. It helps us navigate our future, control our behavior, dream of new possibilities, and guide us throughout our lives.

Meditation strengthens the frontal lobe and shuts down the default mode network, which is the constant chattering of the mind and frees us from being victims of our negative thoughts.

No one can change unless they change their energy and focus. Meditation helps us become aware of our energy and where we are focusing on it. It lets us become familiar with our unconscious thoughts, priming our brains for positive change. During meditation, there are fewer distractions and sensory inputs, and the brain waves change, allowing us to be in the present moment and free from past conditioning.

Initially, many conditioning factors may disturb us while meditating, but we learn not to allow them to affect us. Gradually, our energy stays in the present, and we put a lot of energy into the present moment. As a result, we become more focused and kinder, and the quality of our work improves. We can do more quality work in less time with minimal energy expenditure and distraction.

By investing in ourselves through meditation, we are investing in our future. We become less seduced by past conditioning and start feeling better without any particular reason. Meditation provides us the ultimate freedom from past conditioning and all forms of suffering.

For light, we need a source, but darkness is natural, fighting with darkness is not a solution. The same is true for negative emotions. They are a part of our instinctive nature. Fighting with one negative emotion at a time or suppressing them won't work.

We need to accept them. They are natural, just like gravity, which pulls us down. We only need to make an effort to bring the light of meditation, and with that, the darkness of all lifetime negative emotions washes away, and one is relieved of all the burden of negative emotions.

I hope this understanding helps you continue your meditation journey with ease and joy.

Keep meditating!

Part II:
What Is Meditation

Chapter-I

Meditation- The optimum utilization of the Human Brain - The Neocortex.

Welcome to the first Chapter of our discussion on what meditation is. In this Chapter, we will explore the concept of meditation and its relation to our evolution. To better understand meditation, we will first discuss the triune brain theory. Understanding our fundamental nature is essential for comprehending meditation.

According to the triune brain theory, we have three brain parts. The reptilian brain, also known as the instinctive brain, is the oldest part of our brain, dating back 400 million years. It automatically governs core survival functions such as breathing, heart rate, and pain receptors.

Other living creatures share the same brainstem and cerebellum structure. The reptilian brain is responsible for the fight-or-flight response and cannot distinguish between a real attack and an online game. It triggers the autonomic nervous system and our unconscious mind. Its main functions are food, fight-or-flight, reproduction, sense of pain, and avoiding danger.

The next part of the brain, the mammalian brain or the midbrain, is the emotional brain, which is 100 million years old. It is responsible for eight core emotions: joy, sadness, trust, disgust, etc. This part of the brain plays a significant role in how we learn, store memories, and make judgments. When this part of the brain dominates, our decisions are colored by emotions.

The neocortex is the newest part of our brain, only 4 million years old. It is our conscious mind and can exert control over the other layers of the brain. This part of the brain is only active in heightened awareness. In other situations, our thoughts, decisions, and actions are dominated by the instinctive and emotional parts of our brains.

Our reptilian brain is 400 million years old, and because of it, the fear and threat to life are deeply embedded. This instinctive brain automatically makes us aware of pain or threat, allowing us to avoid it and protect ourselves.

Due to this, most of us are always in survival mode, which is why there is so much stress and anxiety in the life of a modern man. The deep embedding of the reptilian brain is the reason that 80% of our thoughts are negative and related to survival and preparing for future threats, as this is what we have been doing for millions of years, and old habits die hard.

Man has used thinking as a tool for survival, and it has been helpful in allowing us to survive because we can think. Thinking has always been a weapon, and it distinguishes us from animals. Anger, violence, and stress also guard us from danger. Planning is a part of guarding, which is why there is so much future thought, overthinking, worries, and anger in life.

For around 400 million years, we have survived and lived with a reptilian brain that is designed to keep us safe from danger. However, this mechanism can also cause us to focus on negative thoughts and experiences, which can lead to a sense of misery and pain. Unfortunately, we don't have a built-in mechanism to be aware of pleasure when there is no suffering, which can make it challenging to experience joy and happiness in normal conditions. Like we feel hungry, but when we are satiated, do we feel it? No, we don't.

But there is hope. Regular meditation can help us strengthen the neocortex part of our brain, which is responsible for higher-level thinking and consciousness. By focusing our attention and becoming more mindful, we can break free from our animalistic tendencies and experience a greater sense of peace and fulfillment.

Let's take an example of dealing with personal conflict. Imagine a situation in which we are having a heated argument with a relative or some stranger for some reason. Our instinctive brain can trigger a fight-or-flight response, leading to retaliation or withdrawal. This brain is so automatic that we behave like robots, and we don't have any control over our thoughts, emotions, and body.

If the emotional brain is triggered and taken over during the argument, emotions like anger, frustration, hurt, or sadness might surge.

Our emotional brain processes these feelings, making it challenging to think rationally and logically.

But As the argument continues, our neocortex brain engages, allowing us to pause and consider the situation more objectively.

The neocortex enables us to see the bigger picture, understand the other person's perspective, and strategize how to handle the situation constructively.

We use more of the neocortex only if we have meditated well and know how to master emotions.

Mediation is a tool to activate the neocortex of the human brain.

With the practice of meditation, it becomes easy for us to use our neocortex part brain, the human brain, and we behave humanly not based on instinct, the reptilian brain or emotion, the animal brain.

With meditation, we learn to pause, stop, and rationalize a situation.

When we operate on a higher level of awareness, we are no longer solely focused on survival and reacting to our environment. Instead, we can live in the present moment with a sense of bliss and contentment. With practice, we can retrain our brains to focus on the positive and cultivate a more optimistic outlook on life.

Meditation provides us with a new perspective on life, allowing us to see joy in everything around us. It is a state of bliss and joy that is always available to us, even in the midst of challenges and difficulties.

The practice of meditation enables us to break free from our past conditioning and the influences of our reptilian brain and the people around us. By focusing on our internal world, we can cultivate a sense of calm and joy that cannot be disturbed by external factors.

Meditation is a path that we can continue to follow throughout our lives. By staying committed to this journey, we can connect with our deeper core and eventually embody a state of permanent bliss as our natural state of being.

Thank you for considering these insights, and I encourage you to continue your meditation practice.

Keep meditating!

Chapter-2

Meditation- "Chitta vritti nirodha- The cessation of thought and state of relaxation

Welcome to the second chapter of our discussion on what meditation is.

In this chapter, we will understand the nature of the mind and understand meditation as chitta vritti nirodha, the stoppage of thought.

Meditation is a journey within oneself that leads to knowing one's true self. The word "meditation" has its roots in the word "medicine," just as medicine cures the body, meditation cures the mind. To understand meditation better, it is essential to understand what the mind is.

The mind is a result of the coordination of thought impulses throughout various brain regions. Neuroscientifically speaking, the mind is not the brain but rather its product. It is the brain's functioning—gathering, processing, storing, recalling, and communicating information.

Without the brain, there is no mind. Furthermore, the mind is not physically contained within the brain but exists in the form of electric signals that can be detected away from the brain.

The technique of Magnetoencephalography (MEG) is used to map brains activity by recording magnetic fields produced by electrical currents that occur naturally in the brain. During an MEG, the person wears a helmet kept a small distance from the head. The helmet has special sensors that detect the tiny magnetic signals produced by the brain, i.e., thoughts.

Therefore, the mind is not a noun but a verb - it is not a physical entity but a process of thinking and brain functioning that can be recorded. The mind is minding, not just a static thing called "mind."

When we talk about the mind, we refer to a process of thinking within the brain. This process is constantly moving from past to future or future to past, which can create tension and stress.

To cope with this, we often keep ourselves engaged in various activities to avoid becoming aware of this constant movement.

However, if we can decrease this thinking process, we can reach a state of no mind. This means there is no longer any active thinking happening within the brain. This state of no-mind is often achieved through meditation, which allows us to gain mastery over our minds and reduce the constant chatter of thoughts.

In Sanskrit, there is a word for this process of thinking, "chitta." It is important to note that chitta is not the same as the mind but rather a process, i.e., minding.

According to the sage Patanjali, yoga is defined as "chitta vritti nirodha," which means the cessation of thought. The ultimate goal of meditation is to reach a state in which the brain no longer engages in active thinking.

Meditation is often misunderstood as an act of meditating on something, but in reality, it is a state of being. It is a state of no thought and no mind, where there is only emptiness and the witnessing self.

When we examine the mind's nature more closely, we realize it is like a tape recorder, storing memories and past conditioning. The mind is fixated on the past and clings to it, which can cause anxiety when new situations arise.

The mind is constantly in turmoil, and meditation is a way to transcend it and detach ourselves from its grasp. We must learn not to identify with the mind and its constant chatter.

In meditation, we learn to observe our thoughts without getting caught up in them, and eventually, we can experience a state of stillness and tranquility.

Through meditation, we can learn to let go of our past conditioning and create new patterns of thinking and being. We can break free from the constant turmoil of the mind and find peace within ourselves.

This understanding will help you continue your journey of meditation.

We will have more discussion on the nature of the mind and meditation.

Keep meditating!

Chapter-3

Meditation- Technique to come out of the grip of the past, instinctive brain, ego and fear of death.

Welcome to the third chapter of our discussion series on meditation.

In this chapter, we will continue to explore the nature of the mind, constant thinking, and meditation.

We will explore some reasons for the constant movement of the mind and overthinking, and we will all understand meditation as a tool to avoid overthinking.

As discussed in the last chapter, the mind is a process of thinking, and meditation is a state of no thought and no mind. When there are no thoughts, there is pure emptiness, which is the state of meditation.

However, the mind constantly moves from the past to the future and from the future to the past. It is never in the present moment. Meditation is to stay in the present moment effortlessly. We can only experience life in the present moment, but our minds are constantly in motion, causing us to be fully present rarely.

As a result, we miss out on the richness of life and fail to experience things in their entirety. However, by fully experiencing something, we can transcend it and let it go.

Assume a rich man owns the softest bed on earth but can't enjoy its softness or comfort due to overthinking and sleepless nights. Or think of a person sitting in the best and most costly restaurant but can't enjoy food fully due to constant chattering of the mind.

Meditation is a powerful tool that can help us live in the present moment, breaking free from habitual thinking patterns and enabling us to engage with and experience it fully.

Now, we will delve into some reasons why we miss being present and why most of us are constantly thinking.

Our constant thinking is mainly because thinking has become a habit. Out of the 60,000 thoughts we have in a day, approximately 95% are repetitive, and we have grown accustomed to them.

These habitual thinking patterns have become deeply ingrained in us, creating a sense of comfort and familiarity in our daily routines. However, this also means that we may miss out on the present moment as our minds are preoccupied with these habitual thoughts.

Additionally, our instinctive brain, as previously discussed in the triune brain theory, contributes to our constant thinking. The instinctive part of our brain is constantly engaged in planning for the future, avoiding danger, imagining negative situations, and planning for survival.

As a result, out of the 60,000 thoughts we have in a day, approximately 80% of them are negative due to the influence of this part of our brain.

Through meditation, we can activate the neocortex part of our brain, which is responsible for higher-level thinking, and control the instinctive part. Meditation allows us to break free from habitual thinking patterns and helps us be present in the here and now.

It also helps us develop greater awareness of our thoughts and identify and detach from negative thought patterns. By focusing on the present moment, we can experience greater peace, clarity, and connection with the world around us.

Our ego and fear of death also contribute to excessive thinking.

The saying "other is hell" highlights the impact of our ego on our relationship with others. Other people can be a source of emotional or psychological distress, particularly when we become attached to their approval or opinions of us. If we place too much importance on the opinions or actions of others, we may become overly concerned with how we are perceived by them, which can lead to anxiety, stress, and unhappiness.

We often worry about what others might think of us, but the truth is, they're likely preoccupied with their own concerns—perhaps even wondering what we think about them. For example, imagine attending a party where you're self-conscious about your outfit, thinking everyone is judging you. At the same time, others at the party might feel the same about their own outfits or behavior. When we understand this, it becomes clear that most people are too busy with their own thoughts to truly focus on us. So, why waste energy seeking their validation when it's essentially an illusion?

This attachment to external validation ultimately feeds our excessive thinking patterns, creating a vicious cycle of seeking external validation and heightened mental activity.

We also tend to overthink because our thoughts give us a sense of existence. Without any thoughts, we may feel as if we cease to exist, which can trigger our fear of death. This fear of non-existence is a fundamental human fear, and it can contribute to our constant thinking day in and day out.

So, our old habits, instinctive brain, ego, and fear of death can cause constant thinking and turmoil. Excessive thinking drains our energy, akin to a car that is stopped but has its engine running and begins to overheat.

This constant movement of the mind creates tension, and we often try to escape from ourselves. We may search for distractions in alcohol, music, food, or other activities that can occupy us so much that we forget ourselves. However, constantly escaping and occupying ourselves with such activities can lead to even more tension and negative emotions and harm our health badly.

If we become unoccupied, we become conscious of our inner processes, thoughts, and feelings, which may cause a different kind of tension. We are not so worried during the day because we are occupied outwardly. However, when we sit down quietly to meditate, thoughts rush in from all directions, and we feel crowded with thoughts more than before. This is not because of meditation, but thoughts crowd us every moment of our existence. Whenever we sit down, we become conscious of something we have been constantly escaping from.

Meditation is a practice of being fully present and aware. Meditation is witnessing our thoughts and experiences without judgment or attachment. As we develop this ability to witness, the speed of our thoughts naturally begins to slow down.

Through meditation, we can break free from the conditioning and habitual thinking that often dominate our minds. By letting go of our ego and connecting with the present moment, we become more attuned to the world around us and the interconnectedness of all things.

This process can reduce the dominance of our instinctive brain and allow us to let go of negative thought patterns. Ultimately, meditation can help us to find a sense of inner peace and clarity, enabling us to navigate life with greater ease and purpose.

Through meditation, we become thoughtless more often. This is like encountering death, and slowly but surely, our fear of death begins to disappear. As they say, "Who knows how to die can only understand how to live." In meditation, we can start to tap into our eternal nature and truly live every moment. Meditation can be a powerful tool for living a more fulfilling and present life.

I hope this understanding of the nature of the mind and meditation will help you continue your meditation journey.

Keep meditating

Chapter-4

Meditation- Beyond Thinking, Contemplation, Concentration.

Welcome to chapter four of our discussion of meditation. This chapter will delve deeper into the mind and its functioning and help you understand thinking, Contemplation, and Concentration. The mind is a processor of thoughts that operates differently depending on the situation.

The mind works through thinking, Contemplation, and Concentration.

When thoughts are undirected and jump from one subject to another out of associations, it is called thinking. Thoughts go in all directions; they are multidirectional. This is a waste of energy and an ordinary state of mind that leads nowhere and is not useful.

Like some time we think randomly about work, finance, relationships without any purpose.

Contemplation is a step up from thinking and a better state of mind. It occurs when thoughts move in a directed manner, in a particular direction, not through association. It's thinking only about one thing—like relationships or a poet working on poetry.

In Contemplation, the mind is focused on one subject, and no other thoughts are allowed. Thoughts go in one direction. It's a better state of mind than thinking.

The mind works through Concentration. Concentration is neither thinking nor Contemplation. It is the act of staying at one point and not allowing the mind to move at all.

In thinking, The mind moves in all directions without any purpose, but in Contemplation, it is directed toward one subject purposefully. In Concentration, the mind is not allowed to move in any direction and only focuses on one point. For example, a scientist working on an experiment is concentrating and utterly oblivious to everything else.

In ordinary thinking, the mind is allowed to move anywhere, in any direction. In Contemplation, only one direction is open. In Concentration, only one point is open, and there is no direction. Even that point is not open in meditation, and the mind is not allowed to be.

Meditation is the state of no mind; the mind does not do it.

In Concentration, one is oblivious to everything except the object of Concentration. On the other hand, in meditation, one is alert to everything.

It is the highest state of one's existence. In Contemplation and Concentration, the observer becomes absorbed with the object and is not available in the present moment, but meditation is not concerned with the object.

It is concerned with the subject that concentrates and contemplates.

When we contemplate and concentrate, we understand the object of our Contemplation or Concentration. However, in meditation, our awareness extends to the knower, allowing us to understand more about ourselves, the knower. Meditation is not the knowledge of the object outside; it is the knowledge of the knower.

Meditation is not thinking, Contemplation, or Concentration; it is a state of no thought and no movement of mind. In this state, there is no mind, or the mind is calm, still, and free from distractions, allowing us to connect with our innermost being. Through regular practice, we can develop the ability to enter this state at will and experience a profound sense of inner peace and tranquility.

So, Contemplation and Concentration are steps in the ladder of the meditation journey; they are milestones, as explained by Sage Patanjali through Pratyahara and Dharna. They are the preparation for the dhyana but are not the dhyana.

The state of meditation can be compared to the stillness at the ocean's depths. While the surface of the ocean experiences high tides and waves, deep down at the bottom, there is no disturbance or movement. Similarly, when we interact with the external world, our minds can become disturbed with numerous thoughts and worries, but through meditation, we can connect with our deeper state of being, where we are calm, undisturbed, and peaceful.

I hope this understanding will help you to some extent to continue your meditation journey.

Keep meditating!

Chapter-5

Meditation: Observation and witnessing without identification.

Welcome to the fifth chapter of our discussion on meditation.

In this chapter, we will explore the concept of observation and the witnessing self to better understand meditation.

Let's start.

I request that you try some activities now. Are you ready? Ok.

Take a deep breath and gently close your eyes.

Stay and keep breathing.

Now, become aware of the thoughts in your mind.

Can you see the thoughts? Try to increase your awareness. Can you see them now? Try to find out if they belong to the past or future.

Make a note of it.

Now open your eyes; you may have seen the thoughts; some of you may have seen thoughts after some time of closing your eyes, not immediately, why so will discuss later, but all saw some thoughts, right,

Have you ever wondered who was thinking and who saw those thoughts? Who noticed those thoughts?

Take a moment to reflect on this.

What's your answer? Most of the time, people answer that the mind saw or noticed the thoughts.

But it is not so. Because the mind is busy thinking, and every thought you have when you close your eyes is part of the mind, the mind cannot see itself.

Mind is being observed so mind cannot be observer so mind did not noticed or saw thoughts.

Then, who was observing the mind, and who noticed those thoughts?

That observation was done by the witnessing self. The observation is a functioning of the witnessing self, who is available in all of us and is always watching and present.

We will try to understand about witnessing self.

How do we know we exist? When we see something, hear or feel or taste or smell, we know about ourselves, that we exist, and even when we think, it makes us aware of our existence, but when we quiet our five senses and remove all content from the mind? Do you know we can still feel our existence?

This is our witnessing self, the observer, and the state of simply being. Meditation involves observing the activity of the mind and awakening our witnessing self. By practicing various meditation techniques, we can improve our ability to observe and cultivate our witnessing self.

The act of meditation is simply observing our thoughts without judgment or identification, seeing them from a distance.

This observation is not a function of the mind but rather a quality of the witnessing self. As we observe more, we naturally think less.

Thoughts can be compared to uninvited guests; the key is to refrain from entertaining or giving them energy. If we ignore our thoughts, they will not hover around us.

The challenge lies not in our thoughts but in our reaction to their arrival. Indifference is the key to avoiding getting caught up in our thoughts and emotions; meditation can help us cultivate this indifference.

By observing our thoughts and emotions with detachment, we can begin to disidentify ourselves from them and let them go without creating much disturbance. Ultimately, this process can lead us to greater mental clarity and inner peace.

The witnessing self can be compared to a gatekeeper in a gated community; if the gatekeeper falls asleep, unwanted guests can quickly enter the community and disturb its peace. Similarly, if our witnessing self is not awakened, we may experience stress, worry, and negative emotions.

All meditation techniques aim to awaken the witnessing self, allowing us to notice and prevent unwanted thoughts from entering our minds. As we observe our thoughts, they begin to dissipate, giving us greater control over our mental state.

Through this observation, we recognize that our priorities, likes, dislikes, and desires are constantly changing. However, something within us remains unchangeable.

With continued practice, we can begin to disidentify ourselves from our thoughts and emotions, allowing them to come and go without creating much disturbance. Ultimately, this process leads us to connect with our true, unchanging witnessing self.

Through the practice of meditation, our awareness expands slowly, and as it reaches 100%, thoughts start to fade away, leaving only the witnessing self. This state of pure observation is the highest level of meditation, where there are no clouds of thought to obscure the mind, and the sky of consciousness is clear and empty.

In this state, nothing remains to observe except the observer itself. Witnessing cannot be practiced or forced; it is a natural state that arises when the mind is still, and the observer becomes fully present.

Witnessing is the highest possibility of our being.

Meditation is witnessing without identification.

I hope this understanding will help you to continue your journey of meditation.

Keep meditating!

Chapter-6
Meditation is self-remembrance

Welcome to the sixth chapter of our discussion on what meditation is.

In this chapter, we will explore the concept of self-remembrance and its role in helping us cultivate a meditative state. Self-awareness and self-remembrance are central to the practice of meditation.

Let's take a moment to observe our everyday behavior. It becomes evident that external objects often consume our attention—be it people, tasks, or the environment around us. However, the practice of self-remembering introduces a transformative shift. It involves cultivating a dual awareness: one that remains attentive to the external object of focus and simultaneously to ourselves as the observer.

For example, imagine we are in a heated conversation. Typically, our attention might be fully absorbed by the other person's words or our emotional reactions. But with self-remembering, we maintain an inner awareness, a sense of "I am" in the present moment, while still engaging in the dialogue. This subtle but profound awareness creates a space where automatic reactions or past biases do not rule us.

By developing this dual awareness, we can align our actions with clarity and presence rather than being influenced by prejudices or conditioned responses. Over time, self-remembering allows us to navigate life with a sense of grounded authenticity and heightened self-control.

Further, mystics say we are divided selves with many centers. One moment, we love someone; the next, we hate the same person. We are always different. There is no permanent I in ourselves. This illusion of oneness is created by the physical body, by our name.

The very idea of meditation is to help us develop permanent I, and self-remembrance plays an important role. As of now, we are not conscious of ourselves. The very purpose of meditation is to help us become conscious about ourselves, and it's possible through self-remembrance.

We already discussed that, according to the triune brain theory, we have three brains, and we realize that this body functions through these three brains: instinct, emotions, and intellect. Meditation is to observe these functions and distinguish between them, ensuring that most of our actions are guided by intellect and not based on instinct.

As we start to understand ourselves better through self-remembrance, we understand that there are some mechanical aspects of our being that are part of our lives. They are like a hurdle in our observation, and many times, we forget to observe ourselves and fall asleep again. It's because of identification.

We tend to unconsciously fuse our sense of Self with everything we experience—our thoughts, emotions, beliefs, and even passing ideas. This phenomenon, known as identification, blurs the line between who we are and what we observe. For instance, when we feel anger during a disagreement, we often become angry, reacting impulsively and losing sight of the bigger picture. In this state of identification, impartial observation becomes nearly impossible because the object of our focus wholly consumes us.

Consider a scenario where someone criticizes our work. If we identify with our role or output, the criticism feels personal, triggering automatic defensive reactions like anger, hurt, or withdrawal. These responses are mechanical, dictated not by choice but by conditioning. In such moments, identification magnifies the emotional impact and robs us of control over how we respond.

Self-remembrance offers a powerful antidote. It involves cultivating a dual awareness: staying present to the external situation while recognizing oneself as the observer. By remembering, "I am here, observing this," we create a psychological distance from the emotion or belief.

Using the same example, self-remembrance allows you to acknowledge the feedback without feeling personally attacked instead of reacting defensively to criticism. This practice empowers us to choose a clear response rather than emotional reactivity.

Over time, self-remembrance weakens the hold of identification. It helps us see our thoughts and emotions as temporary phenomena rather than absolute truths, enabling impartial observation and thoughtful action. Through this process, we regain autonomy, acting consciously rather than being puppets of our mechanical reactions.

Meditation is having control over the movement of different minds and guiding in a way that helps us be more conscious. Once we have more control over the body and mind, we develop awareness. As of now, our witnessing Self is not awake in us.

With understanding, once we start observing ourselves, we notice that we do not remember ourselves. We also understand that observation is difficult as there is a constant stream of thoughts going on in the background, emotions, and internal talk distracting our attention from observation.

But if we try , we all can remember ourselves for a short time at will because we all have a certain command over our thoughts. If we start remembering ourselves by self-remembering, it paves the way to awareness.

Meditation is a state of total awareness that includes all experiences. Self-remembrance is an essential component of meditation and requires effort and intentionality. By recognizing our mechanical and automated tendencies, we can begin to transcend the limitations of our ego and connect with a deeper sense of meaning and purpose in life. Through self-remembrance, we can become more fully human, more present, and more available to the world around us.

I hope this understanding will help you understand meditation better.

Keep meditating!

Chapter-7

Meditation: The awareness of separateness from the state of waking, sleeping and dreaming.

Welcome to the seventh chapter of our discussion of meditation. In this chapter, we will discuss the different divisions of the mind and how they relate to meditation. According to Yoga, the mind is divided into three states: waking, sleeping, and dreaming. The fourth state, Turiya, is the state of pure awareness.

Waking, dreaming, and in deep sleep we are different people.

In the waking state, our physical body is operative, and we think in terms of physical objects and sensations. We experience the world through our senses and mind, but we are unaware of the self, the knower. In this state, we are conscious through 19 mediums, including the five senses of knowledge, five organs of action, five pranas, and four functions of the psychic organ.

However, in this state, the body and mind are active and transact with the external world, but there is no awareness of the self, the knower. We know about the world but do not know who we really are unless we are awakened in the true sense. The waking state is just another dream.

The second state is the dream state. In this state, the actual physical world is absent, but the mind creates its own world through imagination. The body is a projection of the mind in the dream state. We experience the world created by the mind without the objects of touch or other senses.

Our dreams are made up of impressions from daily activities and suppressed desires. The things, beings, and events of the waking world are reflected in our dreams. It is neither the waking nor sleep state, and there is no knowledge of the self. In this state, the mind is active, but the body is not, so the senses do not take note of the external world. We have no limitations of society or culture. While dreaming, we feel it all to be real.

Then, there is the dreamless sleep state, where there is no awareness of the body or psychological function. All senses stop, and we are free from all experiences. The mind, body, universe, space, and time all vanish. In this state, there is no duality, no ego, and no suffering. We are not even aware of our existence. There is no mind or intellect.

Our awareness continues even during deep sleep, and in the morning, we remember the sleep as relaxing and deep. There is an awareness that operates even in deep sleep, an awareness of the state of relaxed sleep that is available as a memory in the waking state. This awareness, which is conscious even during the dreamless sleep state, is known as Turiya, the "fourth."

Meditation helps one to become aware of the waking, dream state, and even dreamless sleep state. The whole purpose of meditation is to make us aware of Turiya, which is the highest state of awareness.

With meditation, we understand that the mind, body, intellect, and ego are not our true selves. They are constantly changing, and in the dreamless sleep state, they do not exist at all. However, our sense of self remains constant, existing in all three states. In the dreamless sleep state, we exist solely as awareness. If we can exist safely without something, then that something is redundant, and therefore, the body, mind, intellect, and ego are also redundant. Our identification with them is incorrect. We are pure awareness, which exists in all three states.

This true self, unchanging and aware, is known as Turiya, as described in Mandukya Upanishad. When we identify with the body, mind, intellect, and ego, it is due to our ignorance and is the cause of all suffering. The very nature of our true self is Sat Chit Ananda, which means eternal consciousness and bliss. Turiya is the fourth state that goes beyond dreamless sleep, dream, and awakened states; it's always present. No state can exist without Turiya. In this state, there is pure awareness and awareness of the knower.

The awareness of "I am the witness, the knower" remains constant in every activity in all three states. Due to a lack of knowledge of the self, we get identified with whatever we see, but actually, we are the seer, separate from all that is seen.

So, we are not these states but beyond these states. The moment we realize this, we are separate from all of these, and then we begin to realize the fourth. The awareness of separateness is the turiya.

Meditation is the way to realize Turiya, as it removes our false identification with what is seen and keeps us separate from what comes and goes. Identification is the root cause of all suffering. In dreams, we get identified with the dream and experience emotions like fear, stress, and sadness.

However, once we wake up and realize it was just a dream, we become detached and come back to the real world. Similarly, in the waking state, we often get identified with our emotions like hate, anger, and jealousy, and they take control of us. But if we stay connected to our true nature, i.e., Turiya, and not get identified with these emotions, they will not affect us.

Meditation is how to be aware, awake, and not get identified. When we meditate, our mind becomes thoughtless, and we become alert and aware. As the absorption in Turiya increases and we improve in meditation, we realize real peace and bliss.

The journey of becoming aware starts in the waking state and goes through the dream state and then the dreamless sleep state. Once we start seeing these states separately, we can become aware of the fourth state, which is known as Turiya. The ultimate goal of meditation is to aware of Turiya even in dreamless sleep.

Those who achieve this state are considered real yogis, which is why it is said that yogis never sleep. According to mystics, there is fundamentally only one consciousness that appears as the three states of waking, dreaming, and sleeping. Turiya, the fourth state of consciousness, is not something in addition to the other three states but exists in all of them.

Turiya is like a changeless background over which the three states of waking, dream, and dreamless sleep are projected. It's similar to gold, and the three states are like the bangles, ring, and nose pin made of the same gold but in different proportions. So, the three states of waking, dream, and dreamless sleep are mutually exclusive and cannot exist in the presence of the other state. Only Turiya exists in all three states; hence, it is eternal.

When one wakes up, one is aware of the bliss of that is cused by sleep , caused by no experience, so Turiya is eternal bliss. It is a state where one is relaxed, like in deep, dreamless sleep, but simultaneously alert. The mind must be as thoughtless as it is in deep sleep, but one must not be asleep; one must be perfectly alert and aware. When awareness and this thoughtlessness meet, it is meditation.

Meditation is the way to be in a Turiya state; as one's absorption in Turiya increases and one improves in meditation, one realizes real peace and bliss. Once one gets the taste of the joy of meditation, all worldly joy becomes mundane. Meditation helps us realize eternal joy and bliss.

I hope this understanding will help you to some extent to continue your meditation journey.

Keep meditating

Chapter-8

Meditation: Tool to purify our mind & surrender our ego to our higher self.

Namaste and welcome. In this chapter, we will explore the concept of the mind, its parts, and their role in our daily lives. We will also discuss how, if used properly, different parts of the mind can contribute to a meditative state.

According to the Upanishads, the mind is known as antaḥ-karaṇa or the "inner instrument" because it mediates between our inner Self, the physical body, and the external world. The mind has four functions, which are designated in Sanskrit as Manas (mind or conscious mind), Buddhi (intellect), Ahamkara (part of the mind that creates the illusion of self-ego), and Chitta(part of the mind that stores the impression and action of the thought- subconscious mind) These four functions are like spokes on a wheel, with the wheel engaging the world while the center remains still. An imbalance in the four parts of the mind is the primary reason for our disturbed and restless minds.

Manas is the sensory and processing mind that generates likes and dislikes. It perceives through our five senses: hearing, touch, vision, taste, and smell. Manas has no direction and seeks pleasure through the senses.

It control sense and action organs, but if Manas is misguided by Chitta's impressions of past, it tends to surrender to desires. Manas can only control desires if Chitta, Ahamkara, and Buddhi are behaving correctly.

Buddhi is a discriminatory faculty that works through wisdom and analysis. It decides based on past memories using logic. Buddhi is the decision-maker faculty of the mind, and when it is unclouded, it encourages all the other layers to behave proplery. Buddhi is the faculty that is determinant of finding the higher truth and is closest to wisdom.

Chitta is the faculty of the internal instrument where memories and impressions of actions are stored. It is a repository of the past. The intellect consults with Chitta about past actions and consequences and lessons learned and predicts present actions and their consequences. Our actions are decided by the intellect alone, as it rules over the mind.

Next is Ahamkara- the ego, affirmation, assertion, and "I know." The mind, as Ahamkara, is the maker of an "I." With every action, it proclaims, "I am the doer." Our "I" is the identity of a particular body, personality, patterns of thinking, and life. We cling to a limited self with which we identify. Ahamkara collude with Chitta and bring the memories associated with the person's ego. Ahamkara does not let the intellect see the irrationality of those memories, thereby clouding Buddhi.

Suppose Chitta's function is guided by egoistic thoughts produced by Ahamkara. In that case, it is unable to perform properly, and memory storage only brings up sad and painful thoughts that must have hurt one in past. Ahamkara and the memories of Chitta's association is the primary cause of mental problems. The memories stored in Chitta are colored by the 'I-ness' of Ahamkara and the fight for attention. If Buddhi is not operating correctly, these colored impressions drive Manas to take neither healthy nor good actions for the mind. Buddhi can discriminate between right- wrong, good-bad and command all other faculties to make their decisions right.

When the Chitta is purified, Manas is no longer prey to desires. For this reason, yoga emphasizes unclouding Buddhi to make other aspects of the mind function healthily. Patanjali calls this regulating or balancing the core.

If we analyze deeply, we would realize that Manas, Buddhi, Chitta, and Ahamkara are different aspects of the same mind. They are not separate entities; the mind works differently at different times. Sometimes, when it feels arrogant, it works as ego; when it analyzes, it works as intellect. When it simply moves around with many desires of the past, it works as Chitta. Although the mind works differently, it is all one and the same. When the mind is quiet, without any wavering, without intellect, ego, or memories of the past, it is in a pure state of awareness.

Most of the time, our decisions are influenced by society or dominated by our past memories and desires. Although we may know what is good for us, we often fail to listen to our intellect; instead, our chitta or Manas take over. Like how we build muscles to lift heavier weights at the gym, we need to train our intellect to be stronger than our desires and memories.

With regular meditation, we realize that we are stronger than our desires and memories and develop strong willpower. Slowly, our intellect dominates, and we are no longer victims of our chitta and Manas. We can easily regulate our senses and engage our senses in doing things, which can help us easily go into a state of meditation.

Meditation helps us regulate the movement of our minds and gain control over our senses. By meditating, we can overcome our memories and purify our chitta. We are not influenced by our Chitta, the memories of the past, and we surrender our ego to our higher Self.

In the Kathopanishad, the body is compared to a chariot, the senses to horses, the mind to the reins, and the Buddhi to the charioteer. The mind's role in this analogy is to act as the reins that control the senses and guide them in the direction of the charioteer's choice. If the mind is not controlled by the Buddhi, it will allow the senses to roam freely, leading to destruction and suffering.

Therefore, meditation aims to train the mind to be under the control of the Buddhi, guide the senses toward the right path, and lead a peaceful and fulfilling life. Our thoughts and beliefs no longer shape our perception of reality.

Thank you for being part of this journey. I hope that it inspires you to continue your meditation journey.

Keep meditating!

Part III:
How Meditation

Chapter-1

How Meditation: No suppression of thoughts but persuasion.

Welcome to the first chapter of our series of discussion on how to do meditation. To reap the benefits of meditation, it is crucial to understand how to do it properly. In this chapter, we will learn how to proceed in meditation and discuss the nature of the mind.

In our previous discussions on meditation, we have established that it is a state of mind without thoughts. Therefore, the question of how to meditate is essentially asking how to keep the mind unoccupied and free from thoughts. Meditation happens naturally once we learn how to keep our minds devoid of desires, memories, and daydreams. We cannot force it to happen, but we can create the conditions for it to occur.

When I first began meditating, I was taught not to think during the practice. However, I have realized that this approach is not entirely accurate. When we are engaged in doing something, there may not be many thoughts present. But when we sit with the intention of not thinking, thoughts will likely come up, especially when we close our eyes and do nothing. These thoughts may be related to relationships, work, the past, or the future.

However, denying or suppressing these thoughts often invites them back more strongly. This phenomenon is known as the ironic rebound or the white bear problem. It is a psychological process whereby one make deliberate attempts to suppress certain thoughts, which make them more likely to surface. For example, when someone actively tries not to think of a white bear, they may be more likely to imagine one.

Social psychologist Daniel Wegner first identified this phenomenon through thought suppression studies in experimental psychology in 1987. Since then, his findings have guided clinical practice. According to these findings, individuals may try to suppress certain thoughts or feelings, such as dieters attempting to avoid thoughts of junk food, stressed individuals trying to avoid thoughts of their stressors, or people trying to forget past miseries.

However, such attempts to suppress thoughts can often fail and produce the opposite effect. The more we try to suppress certain thoughts, the more they rebound, becoming stronger and more persistent. This is why attempting to forget past miseries can make life even more miserable, and trying to forget someone can lead to them haunting us even more. Thus, attempting to suppress thoughts can often produce the opposite effect and make them rebound more strongly.

Long ago, the psychologist Carl Jung said, "What you resist not only persists but will grow in size."

Suppressing thoughts is not an effective way to get rid of them. Instead, persuasion is required to convince the mind to let go of those thoughts. Fighting against our thoughts only shows our fear and makes the thoughts even stronger. It's like our left hand fighting with our right hand—no hand will win, and we'll only waste our energy in the process, causing more disturbance.

Unfortunately, many people who start meditation without proper understanding often struggle to make it a part of their daily lives. This is because suppression doesn't work. Instead, we should focus on persuasion.

All meditation techniques are methods of persuasion that aim to help the mind reach a point where it can let go of those thoughts.

However, it's important to note that contemplation, concentration, and chanting can actually strengthen the mind or keep it occupied because everything we do is done through the mind. Therefore, doing nothing and not engaging in any ritual is the only alternative left. When we exist and do nothing, we can achieve a state of awareness that is true meditation.

Instead of suppressing our thoughts, we simply become observers or watchers. This is the essence of meditation—the miracle of watching. As our ability to see increases, our thinking decreases. By simply observing our mind, we become more aware of it, and slowly but surely, our mind starts to melt and dissolve.

Therefore, the goal of meditation is not to stop thinking altogether, but rather to observe and acknowledge our thoughts without becoming attached to them. By simply observing our thoughts and allowing them to pass without judgment, we can begin to cultivate a sense of inner peace and stillness. This approach can be a valuable tool for managing stress and anxiety and promoting overall mental and emotional well-being.

There are many methods of meditation, but one thing is common to all of them: witnessing and watching.

I hope this understanding will help you continue your meditation journey.

Keep meditating!

CHAPTER-2

How Meditation: The single pointed focus on sense objects from gross to subtle.

Welcome to the second chapter of our discussion on How to do Meditation. In this chapter, we will discuss how we can improve our focus and awareness so we can watch our thoughts and emotions to reach the state of meditation.

Let's start.

We are composed of five elements—space, air, fire, water, and earth—and have corresponding senses and sense organs that allow us to perceive those elements and the world around us. Our ability to perceive the five elements that exist in the universe is made possible by our five senses. Space, the subtlest element, cannot be touched, seen, tasted, or smelled, but we can hear it, and therefore, the sense of hearing is associated with the space element.

The next subtle element is air, which can only be heard and felt through touch. Thus, the sense of touch is associated with the air element. The fire element is next, which can be heard, felt, and seen, making the sense of vision related to fire. Water, the next subtle element after fire, can be perceived through hearing, touch, sight, and taste, and therefore, the sense of taste is associated with the water element. Finally, the grossest of all elements, earth, can be perceived through all five senses.

We can hear, feel, see, taste, and smell the earth; therefore, the sense of Smell is associated with the earth element. Our senses enable us to make contact with the elements around us. Through our sensory organs, we can perceive the world around us. Billions of sensory neurons work together to create a communication network that sends information from the eyes, ears, nose, tongue, and skin to the brain for processing so our senses allow us to see, hear, feel, taste, and Smell and make our mind run to gratify those senses as per our preferences.

Our minds wander to gratify our senses and are also distracted because they easily attract our attention. However, if we use our senses properly, they can also lead us inward and help us silence the mind. Rather than using our sense of vision to create desires for external experiences, we can use it to turn inward, see inward, and find inner peace.

All senses have the potential to create a calm and peaceful mental state if used properly and turned inward; all senses can be utilized as a tool for achieving a quiet mind. Senses are like doors opening on both sides; it depends on where we want to go.

Sage Patanjali in Yoga Sutras has explained the inward journey of senses and sense withdrawal as Partihara, a preparation for dharna and Dhayan. Every thought and emotion that arises within us has a foundation in the sensory input we receive through our sense organs.

Our past conditioning and habitual behavior patterns often determine our responses to this sensory input. Due to our previous experiences, we are essentially hardwired to react in certain ways.

During meditation, we intentionally create a space to disconnect from the external world and delve deeper. We can use our senses to guide us toward the core of our being, free from external distractions and chaos.

As per the Ashtanga Yoga of Sage Patanjali, pratyahara, i.e., sense withdrawal, is the foundation of internal yoga. It increases the willpower at the level of sense, and the rush of senses towards their objects is brought under control by the practice of pratyahara.

Pratyhara is a kind of contemplation in which we focus only on a particular sense and avoid unnecessary wandering of the mind to other senses.

Pratyahara involves withdrawing the senses, turning attention inward, using the senses as a tool, and detaching from external stimulation of sense gratification.

For the mind to keep senses under control and avoid running here and there for gratification, we all need to work on and improve our intellect so we can use the senses wisely. Through the intellect, we control the mind and senses. Studying books for wisdom and guidance, listening to mystics for inner exploration and inspiration, and having wise company help improve wisdom.

So once our intellect improves, the mind observes and easily controls the senses through the intellect. Once we progress in the practice of pratyahara and dharna, we realize that even the intellect/mind is observed by the witnessing self.

Katho Upanishad deals with the chariot analogy, i.e., the expression of the human body as a chariot.

The body is equated to a chariot where the horses are the senses, the mind is the reins, and the driver or charioteer is the intellect. The passenger of the chariot is the higher self. "So, using this analogy, think of Pratyahara as a way to free ourselves from being victims of our senses.

It's like taking control of a chariot, where our senses are the horses. The practice of Pratyahara allows us to use our intellect as the charioteer. Instead of being pulled in different directions simultaneously by our senses, we use one sense and guide our senses to move inwardly by making conscious choices."

By Training ourselves to focus on gross to subtle elements of our sensory experience, we improve our awareness and have better control over our senses. When we sit for meditation with closed eyes, we can go deeper by becoming aware of our senses. We start with the sense of hearing, being aware of all the sounds around us, far or near, loud or soft. This helps us to connect with our surroundings and become more aware of our external environment.

We then move on to the sense of touch, becoming aware of all the sensations in our body from top to bottom, scanning the whole body. We then focus on the tip of our nostrils with closed eyes or the darkness we see with closed eyes.

As we progress, we become aware of the sense of taste or no taste, and then the most subtle sense, the sense of Smell or no Smell. This journey helps us become more focused and aware of even the most subtle sensations. It is important to note that this process happens without imagination but through pure focus and alertness.

While our mind may wander during meditation, we bring it back to our senses and learn to be present in the moment, moving from gross to subtle sensations. As we become more alert and aware, we can even observe our thoughts without identifying with them.

With practice, we can also become aware of our emotions and gain mastery over them. This allows us to break free from being slaves to our past and surroundings and become a new being with a better understanding of our thoughts and emotions.

So we need to start practicing with a focus on sound, followed by touch, vision, taste, and, lastly, Smell. We can use these senses to go inward instead of outward. So, we learn not to engage with the senses; instead, we use them as a tool to go inward, which reduces the wandering of the mind.

There is a need to train the mind logically so it can focus even on subtle senses. The journey has to begin with gross sensations, sound, touch, vision, taste, and the subtlest sensation, Smell.

With practice, we become aware that all the senses are controlled by the mind, and the mind is the master of the senses. Once we are established in pratyahara, our awareness increases, and later, we become aware of breath and, later, also of thought and emotions.

With practice, slowly, all senses follow the instructions of the mind. This is how contemplating the senses paves the way to dharna, i.e., concentration and dhyana—the meditation. However, the journey is long, and understanding practice matters a lot.

To truly understand this theory, it is essential to practice it; in guided meditation, part of this book will practice and understand it fully.

I hope this understanding will help you to some extent to continue your meditation journey.

Keep meditating!

Chapter-3

How Meditation: The observation of breath- Bridge between body & Mind.

Hello, and welcome to the third chapter of our discussion on How to Meditate.

In this chapter, we will discuss Dharna (concentration) and the benefits of Observing breath to improve our awareness and achieve a state of Dharna.

Dharana is concentration, where we direct our attention to a specific point. This one-pointed focus prepares the mind for the deeper states of meditation.

Dharna diminishes mental chatter and distractions, creating a more conducive environment for meditation. It is crucial for quieting the mind and preparing us for deeper states of awareness. Dharana is a fundamental step in the process of meditation and involves directing and sustaining one's attention on a single point.

Now, we will try to understand how using breath, one of the most popular and widely practiced methods for Dharna, can help us progress in our meditation journey.

"So, using the analogy of Chairot, imagine your intellect as a charioteer in a chariot being pulled in different directions by senses like horses pulling a chariot. Dharna is like taking control of that chariot. So, instead of letting our mind wander around and being pulled by horses in different directions, we use our intellect, the charioteer, to guide the mind and, in turn, all the senses towards one thing that is devoid of sense gratification.

In pratihara, we choose to move the mind in the direction of one chosen sense inwardly at a time, but in Dharna, all senses are moved in a direction and all taken together and not for gratifying sense but focus on a desired object of our choice. In this case, it's focusing all senses on our breath.

The breath is the bridge between the body and mind. The body is gross; we can see it; the mind is subtle; we can't see it; and the breath is in between; we can feel it. By focusing on the breath and watching the breath, using this bridge after practicing Dharna, we create awareness and can watch even subtle thoughts and emotions.

Further, breathing is both a conscious and unconscious process. We don't have to think about breathing all day long. However, we can also choose to focus on our breath and make it a conscious act. Through the practice of Dharna, by becoming aware of our breath, which is both conscious and unconscious, we can become more mindful of the unconscious mind, which is subtler than breath.

With continued practice, we can also learn to observe our emotions, such as anger, envy, and stress. Once we are observers, they no longer affect us, and we become masters of mind and emotions.

Our breath can influence our state of mind during meditation. Depending on our breathing pattern, we can become more alert or relaxed. An active inhale can make us more alert, while a passive exhale can make us more relaxed. A relatively balanced breath can help us achieve a state of balance and calmness. It is important to note that the effects of our breath on our state of mind may vary from person to person, and it may take some experimentation to find the breathing pattern that works best for us during meditation.

Breath is a powerful tool that can help us become more introspective. This awareness can allow us to observe our thoughts without judgment and gain a deeper understanding of our inner self.

Breath is synonymous with life and the flow of prana or life force within us. It is the first act we take on the day of our birth and the last act we take on the day of our death. In between these two moments lies our life, and our breath is a constant reminder of our connection to this life force. Each inhale represents the inflow of life, and each exhale represents the outflow or release of that life force. By becoming aware of our breath, we can gain insight into the nature of life and death and develop a deeper appreciation for the present moment.

Breath always occurs in the present moment; by watching our breath, we can train ourselves to stay in the present.

Focusing our attention on the rhythm and sensation of our breath can help us cultivate mindfulness and awareness of the present moment.

This can help us let go of worries about the past or anxieties about the future and instead focus our attention on the here and now. We train ourselves to live here and now and learn to experience and enjoy life fully.

Watching our breath is an important practice in developing the ability to observe our thoughts. This is because thoughts are often more subtle and difficult to observe directly than the breath. By initially focusing our attention on the breath, we can train ourselves to observe our thoughts more effectively.

As we become more skilled in observing our breath and thoughts, we begin to develop a deeper understanding of ourselves as the observer or witnessing self. With continued practice, we can also learn to observe our emotions, such as anger, envy, and stress, which are often linked to our thoughts.

The practice of observing our thoughts and emotions is not about suppressing or controlling them but rather about cultivating the ability to observe them with pure awareness and alertness. This allows us to use our energy to observe rather than become victims of our thoughts and emotions.

With regular practice, we can develop mastery over our thoughts and emotions and begin to break free from past conditioning and habitual patterns of thinking and feeling. This can lead to more clarity, inner peace, and a more fulfilling and joyful life. When we sit cross-legged with a straight spine, we experience less gravity and spend less energy.

As we focus on observing our breath, the pattern of our breath gradually changes. Since we are not moving the body or the mind, and we are focusing on the breath happening in the present moment, our energy expenditure is minimal. As time passes, our basal metabolic rate - the rate at which our body spends energy on vital functions like circulation, digestion, and respiration - decreases.

This leads to a reduction in our energy requirements, and as a result, our breath slows down further because we do not need as much energy. As our breath slows down, our mind becomes calmer and more peaceful. By focusing on the breath and minimizing our energy expenditure, we can enter a state of relaxation and inner stillness.

This state is conducive to meditation and helps us connect with our inner self, cultivate self-awareness, and develop greater clarity, peace, and well-being.

Breath connects body and mind and its bridge; the day the bridge is lost, the breath stops, and we die. As breath connects body and mind, it significantly impacts both our physiological and psychological state.

Have you observed that when we experience strong emotions such as anger, our breath becomes fast, and our mind becomes disturbed by many thoughts? When we are calm and peaceful, our breath becomes slow and deep, and we have fewer thoughts.

Now I will ask you a question: are you ready?

Ok, we understand that

**fast breath –many thoughts-
Slow breath –Fewer thoughts**

Then, no breath?

I repeat-

**Fast breath –many thoughts-
Slow breath –Fewer thoughts**

No breath?

What's your answer-   No breath is –death, many may have answered – Death   is correct- but it prolong no breath; if it is a short span of no breath – try   another answer-

**Fast breath –many thoughts-
Slow breath –Fewer thoughts**

No breath-?

Now, what's your answer- No thought? Yes, it is correct.

So no breath – No thought and no mind -is our conclusion

Do you know we all can experience this state of no mind through the natural state of no breath?

When we inhale and after inhalation, breath goes in, but before exhalation, it stops, or after exhalation, breath goes out, but before inhalation, breath stops. In these two natural stoppages of breath, the mind disappears, and we reach a state of no thought.

Shall we try – ok, we will try Now-

Sit erect -

Now gently close your eyes- inhale- and exhale.

Now, let it be natural breath. Inhale, feel the breath go in—see before you exhale—before it comes out, it stops.

Now, exhale and see the breath come out. Be aware and know before we inhale that it stops. Try one more time—become aware when the breath stops; there are no thoughts. Try opening your eyes.

By watching the natural gap of no breath, our focus increases, and our perception improves. We slowly also start watching a subtle gap of no thought between two thoughts. In this gap of no breath and no thought, we can connect to our higher self, our observing self, and that is the ultimate goal of meditation.

Breath is a powerful tool in meditation as it is universal and not associated with any particular image or bias. It happens to everyone all the time, making it accessible to all. Using the breath as a focus point, we can train our chattering minds and improve our awareness.

To begin with, observe your breath. Observe the inhalation and exhalation, the sensation of the air moving in and out of your body. As you focus on your breath, your mind will naturally begin to quiet down, and your awareness will increase. With regular practice, you can experience the benefits of meditation, such as reduced stress and anxiety, improved concentration, and increased well-being.

In summary, the breath is a simple yet powerful tool for training the mind and improving awareness in meditation. By focusing on the breath, we can experience the benefits of meditation and cultivate a more peaceful and present state of mind.

We will have more discussion on methods of meditation.

I hope this understanding will help you to some extent to continue your meditation journey.

Keep meditating!

Chapter-4

How Meditation: Controlling the Movement of Eyes: The widow to the Brain.

Welcome to the fourth chapter of our discussion on how to do meditation.

In this chapter, we will learn how to use our eyes as a tool to enter a state of no thought. This is a kind of practice of dharana(concentration), which paves the way to mediation.

Let's start. We human beings are visual creatures, as much of our knowledge comes from what we see and perceive in our surroundings. While other animals, such as dogs, have a keen sense of smell, or bats have excellent hearing, humans are primarily visual beings. What we see has a profound impact on what we do, how we feel, and who we are. Our eyes act as windows to the mind, representing and closely connected with our mental processes. The movements of our eyes reflect the movements of our minds.

Numerous studies have demonstrated that eye movements are closely associated with cognitive processes, including attention, memory, and decision-making. Eye movements reflect specific aspects of brain function, providing insight into our thoughts and desires to others, and they may also actively influence and participate in these processes. The eyes are in constant motion, and with every new thought or emotion, the rhythm of eye movement changes. Each eye movement is linked to a particular thought.

The constant movement of the eyes is our inherent characteristic.

If we don't move our eyes and pause, pausing at a particular point creates the potential for inward movement and the observation of one's internal state. When we are not seeing others, we can see ourselves. Whenever we recall memories from the past or plan for the future, our eyes tend to move to the left or right, indicating that eye movements are closely linked to our thought processes.

Do you want to see how your eyes are associated with thoughts and memory? Try now. Take a deep breath. Try remembering what dinner you had last night. Try to remember the vegetables you had for dinner. Now, become aware of how your eyeball has moved, to right or left. Note it- did you notice?

Now again, try: Just imagine where you will be tomorrow at this time— in the office, at home, or anywhere. Just imagine. Notice your eyeball. Did you notice? As we think of the past or future, the eyeball moves accordingly. We can't think without moving the eyeball. Even during our dreams at night, the eyeball moves. Dreaming again is a thinking state of our mind, and the movement of our eyeballs reflects our thoughts in a dreaming state.

When our eyeball moves to the left, we go to the past; when it moves to the right, we go to the future; it may happen the other way around, depending on individuals. When our eyeball does not move either to the left or right and remains centered, we create a possibility of staying in the present.

In essence, our eyeballs' movement mirrors our mind's movement.

While it is not possible to stop the movement of the mind, we can control the movement of our eyeballs. Concentrating or fixing our gaze internally at the tip of our nostrils or doing trataka can be immensely helpful in achieving this goal. Try again with me to have a taste of no thought. Take a deep breath, sit erect, and gently close your eyes.

Now, fix both eyeballs on the tip of your nostril. Ensure you are not moving your eyeball. Use willpower and make an effort. We all can do it.

Now observe when the eyeball does not move; there are no thoughts. We are not doing anything with thoughts; instead, we avoid eye movement. Become aware that if any thought has come, the eyeball moves. Experience it and make a note of it.

Good. I hope you got some taste. Now, open your eyes.

With regular practice of dharna, we can prevent our eyes from wandering and instead focus them on a fixed point, ultimately gaining mastery over the movement of our mind. Excessive exposure to various electronic gadgets like mobile phones, laptops, TVs, and computers can strain our eyes and exhaust our brains.

It is crucial to take breaks and allow our eyes and, in turn, brains to rest by simply sitting and observing. By observation and practicing meditation, we can experience greater joy and peace.

Thank you for your time, and I hope this understanding will encourage you to continue your meditation journey.

Keep meditating!

Chapter-5

How Meditation: The observation of mind i.e. the process of thinking.

Hello, and welcome to the fifth chapter of our discussion on how to do a meditation series. In this chapter, we will discuss how observing the mind can quiet its activity and how pratyahara(contemplation) and dharna(concentration) prepare us for meditation.

We know there are five senses, and the mind connects and harmonizes these senses, acting as the master of all. If we slowly and gradually examine the mind sitting and watching, the birth of the witnessing self happens, or the witnessing self is awakened.

This witnessing self observes the mind and the intellect.

If we analyze, we understand that the mind thinks while our witnessing self observes our thoughts. Watching the senses in contemplation, which is practicing pratyahara, and by watching the breath or fixing the eyeball on the tip of the nostril through concentration, which is dharana, we train ourselves for the practice of dhyana, the meditation, where we awaken our witnessing self and watch our mind—the thoughts, which is more subtle than watching the senses and breath.

So, using the Chairot analogy, imagine the passenger or owner of the chariot as our witnessing self. When the owner is not there or is sleeping, there is a chance that the charioteer may have personal preferences. If the chariot is not being taken in the right direction or is moved slowly or fast, then dhyana is like awakening the sleeping owner and making the charioteer aware of the presence of the owner of the chariot.

The very awareness of the presence of the chariot owner makes the charioteer's mind or intellect conscious of moving in the right direction.

Why did this happen? We will discuss more about it.

We know that we tend to behave differently when we know we are being observed. Similarly, when the mind is being watched, it changes its behavior. Our mind becomes quiet, and the wandering disappears.

Have you ever observed how small kids behave in a class when the teacher is not present? They often engage in all sorts of mischievous activities, shouting and playing around. However, if kids know the teacher is watching them from the window, their behavior changes immediately.

They become more orderly and quiet, knowing that they are being observed. What if even teachers do not behave in an orderly manner? Then there is the principal; the very presence of the principal in his office brings discipline to the whole school. So children can be compared to senses, teachers to mind, and principals to witnessing self. Daily meditation practice, where we sit for some time, can be compared to daily school prayer, where children and teachers attend prayer with the principal. All are made aware that the principal is available in school, which means witnessing self is there so mind and sense behave properly the whole day.

Have you heard about the famous double-slit experiment in quantum physics? According to this experiment, particles such as photons, electrons, and atoms behave differently when observed. When bombarded on a photographic plate, they suddenly stop behaving like waves and start behaving like particles in the presence of an observer. So, the presence of an observer changes their nature, and they start behaving like particles in a disciplined manner instead of a wave, which is disorderly.

Similarly, when our witnessing self observes the mind during meditation, the wandering stops, and the mind becomes silent.

Try one activity with me to better understand why thought stops or is reduced on observation. Are you ready? Gently close your eyes and take a deep breath. Now, see what the next thought in your mind is. Try to identify the very next thought that arises in your mind. Stay alert and note that initial thought. Now, gently open your eyes. What did you notice immediately? Some of you were blank for some time, right? There were no thoughts. You went to the state of no thoughts for a few seconds. When we can experience the state of no thought for a few seconds with practice, we can prolong it.

This is what meditation does.

Do you know why it happened?

When we start observing our minds, the energy that was previously used for thinking is redirected to observing. We do not have the energy to think and divert ourselves to watching, which results in the stoppage of thoughts.

The same happens when we watch our senses in pratyahara (contemplation) and our breath in dharna(concentration). The energy previously spent on thinking is now utilized to observe our senses and breath, resulting in fewer thoughts. This is how observation helps in achieving a state of meditation.

The very nature of the universe is entropy, disorder, and chaos, which is reflected in our minds as well. It's in our nature to prefer disorder, which is why there is so much restlessness and chaos in our minds. By meditating regularly, we can improve our awareness and bring order to our minds. We come to realize that we are observers, and as our observing capacity increases, our thinking decreases.

When there is a hundred percent observation, the thinking stops.

By cultivating watchfulness, we can transform our mental habits and patterns, leading to greater clarity, peace, and happiness in our daily lives.

I hope this understanding will help you to continue your journey of meditation.

Keep meditating!

Part IV:
Benefits of Meditation

Chapter-1

Meditation Strengthen key brain region: Harness the power of meditation to make your brain smarter, happier & healthier.

1. **Meditation brings balance between Left Brain and Right Brain:**

   Meditation has numerous benefits, and one of the most notable is its effect on balancing the left and right hemispheres of the brain. Research has shown that regular meditation can increase connectivity and communication between the two brain hemispheres, resulting in a more integrated and cohesive brain function.

   Balancing the left and right hemispheres of the brain can lead to numerous benefits, including improved cognitive abilities such as enhanced creativity, better problem-solving skills, and increased focus and concentration. Additionally, a more balanced brain function has been linked to better emotional regulation and an increased sense of well-being.

   "corpus callosum (CC)," **is thought** to be responsible for the Einstein's creativity.

Several studies have explored the impact of meditation on brain connectivity and integration. Functional magnetic resonance imaging (fMRI) studies have shown that long-term meditation practitioner's exhibit increased connectivity between different brain regions involved in attention, self-awareness, and emotional regulation.

A study published in the journal Frontiers in Psychology in 2018 investigated the effects of meditation on interhemispheric connectivity—the communication between the left and right hemispheres of the brain. The study found that experienced meditators showed increased interhemispheric connectivity compared to non-meditators.

Recent studies have shown that meditation can specifically improve the function of the **corpus callosum**, the bridge that connects the left and right hemispheres of the brain. This can lead to increased creativity, problem-solving ability, and improved communication and interpersonal skills.

2. Meditation help one deal with the Loneliness:

Loneliness is a growing concern in today's society and recent studies have shown the beneficial effects of meditation in dealing with loneliness. A study published in the prestigious 'PLOS Medicine' journal, which involved over 300,000 participants, found that individuals with strong social relationships, both in terms of quality and quantity, lived 50% longer and reported higher levels of happiness than those who were socially isolated.

Furthermore, research conducted by Dr. Andrew Newberg at the University of Pennsylvania found that meditation can have a profound effect on the **parietal lobe** of the brain, the area responsible for processing three-dimensional space and our sense of self in relation to others. During meditation, the parietal lobe activity reduces significantly, leading to a sense of connectedness with others and a reduction in feelings of loneliness and social isolation.

One study published in the journal "Psycho neuroendocrinology" in 2012 examined the effects of a mindfulness meditation program on loneliness and inflammatory responses in older adults. The study found that participants who engaged in mindfulness meditation experienced reduced feelings of loneliness and decreased pro-inflammatory gene expression compared to a control group.

Additionally, a study published in the journal "Mindfulness" in 2015 investigated the effects of a mindfulness-based intervention on loneliness and social connectedness. The findings indicated that the mindfulness intervention significantly reduced loneliness and increased social connectedness among participants.

These findings suggest that meditation can be a powerful tool for improving social connections and reducing feelings of loneliness. Meditation helps calm the activity in the parietal lobe, so individuals can experience a greater sense of interconnectedness with others, leading to improved well-being and a sense of belonging.

3. Meditation Ends Depression:

Major depressive disorder (MDD) is a common mental health condition affecting 1 in 15 people at any given time. Fortunately, meditation has been found to be a helpful tool in managing depression.

Recent research has shown that regular meditation practice can lead to changes in the brain that may be beneficial for individuals with depression.

A 2008 study published in the Neuro image Journal showed that participants who practiced meditation for just 8 weeks experienced significant growth in neural thickness, density, and overall size in the left and right **hippocampi** of their brains. The hippocampus is a region of the brain that plays a critical role in regulating mood and emotion.

Another meta-analysis published in JAMA Psychiatry in 2019 analyzed 18 studies and concluded that mindfulness-based interventions, including meditation, were associated with significant reductions in depressive symptoms compared to control conditions.

Furthermore, a study published in JAMA Network Open in 2020 explored the effects of a mindfulness-based stress reduction program on patients with moderate to severe depression. The study found that the mindfulness intervention significantly reduced depressive symptoms, with approximately half of the participants experiencing a clinically important improvement.

Overall, these findings suggest that meditation can be an effective tool for managing depression. Regular practice of meditation can lead to changes in the brain that may be beneficial for individuals with depression, and meditation can be just as effective as medication in treating depression.

4. Meditation Improves Memory and Learning:

Recent scientific findings have shown that meditation can positively impact memory and learning. Dr. Sara Lazar and her colleagues at Harvard University, who have been studying the meditating brain for decades, have made several discoveries related to the benefits of meditation.

One of the most significant findings is that meditation can increase the thickness of the **hippocampal cortex,** a part of the brain that is critical for learning and memory. Dr. Lazar's research has shown that regular meditation can sculpt the brain's structure to enhance its ability to process and retain information.

A 2013 study published in the journal PLOS ONE found that participants who underwent an eight-week mindfulness meditation program improved working memory capacity compared to a control group.

Another study published in 2016 in the journal Consciousness and Cognition investigated the effects of meditation on learning and memory. The researchers found that participants who engaged in meditation training demonstrated enhanced episodic memory, which involves recalling specific events and experiences.

Furthermore, a 2021 study published in the journal Psychological Science found that meditation can improve working memory, which allows us to hold and manipulate information in our minds for short periods. The study revealed that individuals who practiced meditation had better working memory performance than those who did not.

These findings suggest that meditation can be a valuable tool for improving memory and learning. By reshaping the structure of the brain, meditation can enhance its ability to process and retain information, and improve working memory

5. Meditation Makes one Kind, Compassionate and Happier:

Recent scientific findings have confirmed that meditation can make us kinder, more compassionate, and happier. A brain imaging study conducted by researchers at the University of British Columbia observed that when individuals donate to charity, the pleasure center of their brain, the **insular cortex,** lights up.

Moreover, many of history's greatest humanitarians were also meditators. This is not a coincidence, as meditation has been found to enhance feelings of compassion and connectedness to others.

Recent research has shown that true happiness does not come from material possessions or experiences, but from practicing compassion and generosity towards others. When we help others without expecting anything in return, when we are kind simply for being kind, and when we view others as extensions of ourselves, we experience a deeper sense of happiness and fulfillment.

A study published in Psychological Science in 2020 explored the link between meditation and prosocial behavior. The researchers found that individuals who engaged in meditation practices, such as loving-kindness meditation, were more likely to display acts of kindness and generosity towards others.

Furthermore, investigations into the impact of meditation on happiness and well-being have consistently shown positive outcomes.

A meta-analysis published in the Journal of Happiness Studies in 2021 examined multiple studies on the effects of meditation on subjective well-being. The analysis revealed that meditation interventions were associated with increased levels of happiness, life satisfaction, and overall well-being.

Overall, the latest scientific findings reaffirm that meditation can effectively cultivate kindness, compassion, and happiness. Through regular practice, individuals can experience changes in brain activity related to empathy and compassion, engage in more pro social behavior, and enjoy enhanced subjective well-being.

By incorporating meditation into their lives, individuals have the potential to create a positive ripple effect, fostering a kinder, more compassionate, and happier society.

6. Meditation boosts Emotional Quotient:

EQ is an individual's ability to make moral decisions.

"IQ gets you hired. EQ gets you promoted." — Time Magazine.

Emotional Quotient (EQ), also known as emotional intelligence, encompasses an individual's ability to perceive, understand, and manage their own emotions while effectively navigating social interactions. The latest scientific findings indicate that meditation can boost an individual's Emotional Quotient (EQ).

A 2016 study conducted by Spanish and German researchers found that after just 40 days of mindfulness training, meditators exhibited significant increases in the "internal consistency" of their **temporoparietal junction (TPJ)**. This brain region is associated with empathy, perspective-taking, and the ability to understand the mental states of others.

Meditators have long been associated with emotional balance and self-control, and these findings provide scientific evidence for these claims.

Individuals with high EQ are often more successful in their personal and professional lives, as they are able to navigate complex social situations, build strong relationships, and make ethical decisions.

A comprehensive review of studies published in 2021 analyzed the effects of various meditation practices on emotional intelligence. The findings consistently indicated that meditation interventions, such as mindfulness and loving-kindness meditation, were associated with significant improvements in EQ. Participants demonstrated enhanced emotional awareness, empathy, emotional regulation, and social skills after engaging in regular meditation practice.

Neuro scientific research using advanced brain imaging techniques has provided insights into the underlying mechanisms through which meditation impacts EQ. Studies have shown that long-term meditators exhibit structural and functional changes in brain regions associated with emotional processing and regulation, including the prefrontal cortex and insula. These changes contribute to heightened emotional self-awareness, increased empathy, and improved emotional regulation abilities.

Furthermore, a randomized controlled trial published in 2022 investigated the effects of a meditation-based intervention on EQ in the workplace. The study revealed that employees who participated in a workplace meditation program experienced significant improvements in their EQ scores compared to the control group. These improvements were accompanied by enhanced communication skills, better conflict resolution, and improved job satisfaction.

The latest scientific findings support the notion that regular meditation practice can contribute to the development and enhancement of EQ. By cultivating emotional intelligence through meditation, individuals can improve their self-awareness, empathy, and social skills, leading to more successful interpersonal relationships and greater overall well-being in personal and professional contexts.

7. Meditation reduce Stress response and ends Anxiety:

In 2011, researchers at Massachusetts General Hospital conducted fMRI brain scans on 51 adults both before and after an 8-week training program in mindful meditation. The results revealed that individuals who practiced meditation effectively subdued the "electrical activity" within their primitive amygdala. Consequently, they experienced fewer signals of anxiety, worry, and fear in their minds.

The remarkable finding that shook the scientific community was that these participants reduced the size and volume of their **amygdala** significantly in less than two months, defying the notion that such changes require years of practice.

Despite living in modern cities where we are free from the threats of lions and tigers, our brains remain wired, much like those of our Stone Age ancestors. The daily challenges of jobs, financial difficulties, and relationship issues can still trigger our fight-or-flight fear response.

Meditation serves as a tool allowing us to experience a state of greater calm and freedom from worries. Recent scientific research has provided further evidence of the beneficial effects of meditation on reducing stress and anxiety.

In a study published in 2022, researchers from multiple institutions conducted a systematic review and meta-analysis of 47 randomized controlled trials involving over 3,500 participants. The findings consistently demonstrated that meditation practices, such as mindfulness meditation, were associated with a significant reduction in stress levels and symptoms of anxiety. The analysis also revealed improvements in measures of psychological well-being and overall mental health.

Neuroscientific studies have shed light on the underlying mechanisms through which meditation exerts its positive effects. Functional magnetic resonance imaging (fMRI) studies have shown that regular meditation practice can lead to structural and functional changes in brain regions involved in emotion regulation, such as the amygdala and prefrontal cortex. These changes result in decreased reactivity to stressors and improved emotional resilience.

Moreover, research suggests that meditation promotes the activation of the parasympathetic nervous system, responsible for the "rest and digest" response, and reduces the activity of the sympathetic nervous system, associated with the "fight or flight" response. This shift in autonomic nervous system activity contributes to a state of deep relaxation, reduced physiological arousal, and a decrease in stress-related symptoms.

The latest scientific findings support the notion that meditation serves as an effective tool for managing stress and anxiety in our modern lives. By incorporating regular meditation practice into our daily routines, we can cultivate a greater sense of calm, enhance emotional well-being, and develop the resilience necessary to navigate the challenges of our fast-paced world.

8. Meditation ends insomania:

Meditation ends insomnia:Insomnia is a widespread problem that affects the lives of millions of people around the world. It can be challenging to achieve the deeper levels of sleep, such as REM sleep, which is essential for detoxifying blood, repairing organs, healing wounds, renewing cells, building muscle tissue, and other critical functions.

The brainstem's **"Pons"** region regulates the primary dreamtime chemical, melatonin. In 2014, a team of Harvard and Stanford University researchers discovered that meditation can strengthen and enlarge the sleep-centered Pons region through the power of neuroplasticity.

More recent studies have also shown that mindfulness meditation can improve sleep quality and reduce insomnia symptoms. For instance, a 2021 randomized controlled trial published in the Journal of Sleep Research found that participants who received mindfulness meditation training experienced significant improvements in both subjective and objective measures of sleep quality.

By reshaping the brain's structure and function, meditation can help individuals achieve deep and restful sleep, which can lead to a range of physical and mental health benefits.

9. Meditation can makes one intelligent, smart, and Healthy:

Upgrading the prefrontal cortex opens a whole new dimension of powerful benefits: less anxiety, less depression, more success, more processing power, better decision-making, better health, stronger willpower, higher IQ, and so on.

A landmark study by Harvard neuroscientists found that experienced meditators had much more neural density, thickness, folds, and electrical activity within the prefrontal cortex. That's also what made Albert Einstein's brain so unique. Recent studies have further confirmed the positive effects of meditation on the prefrontal cortex. In 2018, a team of researchers from the University of California, Los Angeles, found that just four sessions of meditation led to increased activity in the prefrontal cortex, as well as improved connectivity between this region and other areas of the brain involved in emotional regulation and cognitive control.

Moreover, another study published in the Journal of Neuroscience in 2020 found that long-term meditation practice is associated with greater thickness and volume of the **prefrontal cortex.** The researchers also found that these structural changes were linked to improved attention control and emotional regulation.

The prefrontal cortex is crucial for many higher-order cognitive functions, including decision-making, planning, attention, and working memory. Therefore, by boosting the growth of this region through regular meditation practice, we can potentially improve our overall cognitive abilities and emotional well-being.

10. Meditation can be viewed as a workout for the brain.

The key regions of the brain that are impacted during meditation bring about significant changes in our psychology, affecting the way we think and respond to stimuli. Simply reading and understanding concepts is not enough to effect lasting change within ourselves. Instead, we must work on the very foundations of our being by altering the physiology of the brain.

Through meditation, we can achieve this goal and bring about a transformation in our lives.

CHAPTER-2

Meditation Develops Prefrontal Cortex

Neuroscientists have found that the more meditation experience a person has, the more highly developed his/her prefrontal cortex is.

1. **Meditation improves intuition and Help in making better Decision:**

    Intuition and making better decisions are essential for success, including in business leadership. In a study involving thirty-six CEOs, 85% identified "intuition" or "gut feeling" as the most critical component of their decision-making process. The **ventromedial prefrontal cortex (vmPFC)** has been identified as a key brain region involved in intuition. Researchers from the University of Iowa have referred to it as the "axis of intuition."

    A study conducted by Wake Forest University in 2014 examined the effects of mindfulness training on the brain. They found that just four days of mindfulness training led to increased activity and interconnectivity within the vmPFC of 15 participants.

    Further, a study published in Scientific Reports in 2021 (Creswell et al.) investigated the effects of a brief mindfulness training session on intuition and decision-making. The researchers found that participants who underwent mindfulness training exhibited enhanced intuition and made more advantageous decisions than those in the control group. The study suggests mindfulness meditation can improve intuitive decision-making by increasing present-moment awareness and reducing cognitive biases.

These recent scientific findings support that meditation can improve intuition and improve decision-making. Meditation may help individuals tap into their intuitive capacities by cultivating present-moment awareness and enhancing neural connectivity, leading to more informed and advantageous decisions. Meditation can serve as a tool to amplify the subtle cues from our inner selves and guide us towards a more fulfilling life. We can gain clarity and make more informed decisions by quieting the mind and becoming attuned to our intuition.

Incorporating meditation into our daily routine can support the development of intuitive abilities, providing a valuable resource for making better decisions in both personal and professional life.

2. Meditation is the ultimate Guide to Willpower:

Stanford University researcher Walter Mischel, known for his famous marshmallow test, stated that the ability to manage hot emotions has broader implications beyond just resisting immediate temptations. It can also enable individuals to focus on studying for important exams, save money for the future, and make long-term beneficial choices.

The **dorsolateral prefrontal cortex (DL-PFC),** located deep behind the forehead, is associated with willpower and self-control in the brain. Italian neuroscientists conducted a study examining the brains of individuals new to meditation before and after an eight-week mindfulness course (Tomasino et al.). The researchers made several remarkable discoveries. One of their findings was that the meditators exhibited strengthened dorsolateral prefrontal cortex(es).

Meditation can enhance willpower and enable individuals to engage in activities they may initially resist but recognize as necessary, such as regular exercise, waking up early in the morning, and maintaining a healthy diet.

A study by researchers at the University of California, Santa Barbara in 2021 (Tang et al.) investigated the relationship between meditation, the dorsolateral prefrontal cortex (DL-PFC), and self-control. The researchers found long-term meditation practice was associated with structural changes in the DL-PFC, indicating enhanced connectivity and functional efficiency.

These changes were linked to improved self-control abilities, including resisting immediate gratification and making long-term beneficial choices.

The recent scientific findings support the idea that meditation can strengthen the dorsolateral prefrontal cortex, improving willpower and self-control. By engaging in regular meditation practice, individuals can potentially increase their ability to overcome temptations, engage in healthy behaviors, and make decisions aligned with their long-term goals.

By nurturing mindfulness and strengthening the dorsolateral prefrontal cortex through meditation, individuals can cultivate the inner resources necessary to resist distractions, make conscious choices, and take actions that lead to personal growth and well-being.

3. Meditation improves Grit Scale(Passion and Perseverance):

Duckworth and colleagues interviewed top performers in many fields, including investment banking, art, journalism, academia, medicine, and law. Again and again, grit was found to be the most accurate "high achievement" predictor. Grittiest" brain region is the "**anterior cingulate cortex**" **(ACC)** pain resistance, willpower, motivation, focus, and emotional resilience are among the ACC's wide range of functions.

The University of Montreal researchers (Grant et al) compared the brains of 17 experienced meditators to 18 "normal" brains. The meditators' brains had much "thicker" gray matter in the anterior cingulate cortex (ACC).

One study published in the journal "Mindfulness" in 2016 examined the relationship between meditation and grit among college students. The study found that higher levels of mindfulness, which is cultivated through meditation, were associated with greater perseverance and self-regulation, which are key components of grit.

Another study published in the "Journal of Occupational Health Psychology" in 2018 investigated the effects of mindfulness meditation on workplace performance and grit among employees. The findings indicated that mindfulness meditation training was associated with increased levels of grit, as well as improved job performance and work engagement.

4. Meditation restores the Power of Now and Transforms the Monkey Mind:

The default mode network (DMN) is an active network of interacting brain regions when a person is not focused on the outside world. When the brain has nothing to do, its "Default Mode Network (DMN)"(Monkey mind) switches on. Recent research has associated hyperactivity of the DMN with diseases like depression, anxiety, and schizophrenia with the DMN.

As the "**Posterior Cingulate Cortex**" **(PCC)** is directly linked to our, Default Mode Network (DMN), strengthening this region is the secret to making our monkey mind docile, gentle, and submissive. Luckily, that's exactly what meditation does. Among four key brain regions, Harvard University researchers (2011, Hölzel et al) discovered that meditation dramatically increases the Posterior Cingulate Cortex's "gray matter concentration.

A study published in "Frontiers in Human Neuroscience" in 2018 investigated the effects of meditation on the Posterior Cingulate Cortex, a key region within the DMN. The researchers found that individuals who practiced mindfulness meditation exhibited increased gray matter density in the PCC, suggesting structural changes in this region. These changes were associated with improved attention and self-awareness.

Additionally a study published in the journal "NeuroImage" in 2019 examined the relationship between meditation and the DMN. The researchers found that long-term meditators showed decreased functional connectivity within the DMN, indicating a reduced tendency for mind-wandering and self-referential thinking. This suggests that meditation may help in quieting the mind and reducing the "monkey mind" phenomenon.

These findings suggest meditation can have positive effects on the DMN, including reduced mind-wandering, structural changes in the PCC, and improved attentional processes.

5. Meditation help one to achieve the State of Flow:

As per Dr. C mihályi flow is "being completely involved in an activity for its own sake. Time flies. Every action, movement, and thought follows inevitably from the previous one. Your whole being is involved, and you are using your skills to the utmost. Runners High, in the zone, are other words used for state of flow.

There are four states in flow- Struggle, release, flow, and recovery. In 2013, Belgian researchers examined 27 Parkinson's patients before and after an 8 week mindfulness meditation . In addition to other improvements, meditation increased **gray matter density (GMD).** Creativity and happiness are just the first two drops in an ocean of benefits. One is in the highest state of creativity and focus, which helps to be with work in hand and in the present moment.

A study published in the journal "Frontiers in Psychology" in 2015 investigated the effects of mindfulness meditation on flow states in athletes. The researchers found that athletes who regularly practiced mindfulness meditation reported higher levels of flow experiences during their sport activities compared to those who did not practice meditation.

Further, a study published in the journal "Mindfulness" in 2018 explored the relationship between meditation and flow experiences in a non-athletic population. The researchers found that individuals who regularly practiced meditation reported higher flow experiences in their daily lives compared to non-meditators. They also found a positive association between mindfulness and flow experiences.

These studies suggest that there may be a positive relationship between meditation and the state of flow. Regular meditation may enhance individuals' ability to enter a state of flow, and experience heightened focus, concentration, and immersion in their activities.

Chapter-3

Meditation helps in: Longevity, Life Extension, & Anti-Aging.

1. Meditation helps us live longer:

Meditation has been found to have potential benefits for longevity, and recent scientific research has shed light on its effects on nitric oxide, a potent molecule associated with various health benefits and anti-aging effects. In 1992, the scientific community recognized nitric oxide as the "Molecule of the Year," and in 1998, three scientists were awarded the Nobel Prize in Physiology for their groundbreaking research on its functions in the human body.

Nitric oxide plays a crucial role in several essential processes within the body, including blood pressure regulation and immune system signaling. Unfortunately, by age 40, we lose 50%, and by 60, we lose 85% of our ability to produce Nitric Oxide. This is one of the main reasons why, after 40, we tend to gain weight and develop high blood pressure and insulin resistance, fatigue, and brain fogginess. We all need to restore Nitric Oxide to achieve optimal health.

Studies have indicated that increased nitric oxide levels can contribute to longevity and well-being. For instance, a 2007 study conducted by scientists from the Cleveland Clinic and Case Western Reserve University discovered that meditation can stimulate a more than 1,000% increase in nitric oxide levels within the body.

Further, a 2005 study published in the American Journal of Cardiology demonstrated improved endothelial function in patients with coronary heart disease after a three-month meditation program. Enhanced endothelial function is associated with increased nitric oxide production and improved vascular health.

Additionally, the study published in the Journal of Alternative and Complementary Medicine 2008 showed that a three-month meditation program reduced oxidative stress and increased antioxidant activity in participants. Study suggests that meditation may indirectly contribute to increased nitric oxide levels.

These findings support the notion that meditation has the potential to positively impact nitric oxide production through its effects on endothelial function and oxidative stress. By enhancing the production of this significant molecule, meditation has the potential to exert notable effects on our health and lifespan. Therefore, meditation is increasingly recognized as an essential practice for individuals seeking to extend their lives and improve their overall health.

2. Meditation Can Make us Look Young:

Recent scientific research suggests that meditation has the potential to slow the aging process. Stress is known to accelerate aging, but studies have revealed that meditation may positively impact counteracting this effect. In 2011, researchers at the University of California-Davis examined the white blood cells of 30 individuals before and after a three-month meditation retreat. The study findings indicated that the individuals who practiced meditation had approximately 40% more **telomerase** units per 10,000 cells" compared to the control group.

A study published in the journal Psychoneuroendocrinology in 2020 explored the impact of a brief mindfulness meditation intervention on cellular aging markers. The study involved 64 healthy adults who participated in a three-day mindfulness retreat. Before and after the retreat, participants' blood samples were collected to measure markers of cellular aging, including telomere length and telomerase activity.

The findings revealed that after the three-day mindfulness retreat, participants showed significant increases in telomerase activity compared to baseline. This research suggests that even a short-term mindfulness meditation intervention can have positive effects on cellular aging markers.

Telomerase is an enzyme that helps maintain the length of telomeres, the protective caps at the end of chromosomes. Longer telomeres are associated with improved cellular health and longevity. In addition, the studies also found that individuals with higher levels of mindfulness prior to the retreat had more significant increases in telomerase activity.

Interestingly, lobsters, known for their exceptional longevity, produce abundant telomeres throughout their lives. This continuous production of telomeres contributes to their ability to live well over 100 years. By promoting the production of telomerase and protecting telomeres, meditation may slow down the biological clock and help us maintain a youthful appearance and feel younger.

3. Meditation's ultimate guide to longevity:

Glutathione, a crucial antioxidant in our body's cells, is vital in combating free radicals and maintaining overall health. Glutathione plays a helper role for many critical enzymes, fights cancer, boosts T-cells, shields environmental toxin damage, and guards against drug resistance while supercharging immunity. However, research has shown that as we age, our levels of Glutathione tend to decline, potentially due to decreased body production. This decline in glutathione levels is associated with various health issues and accelerated aging. Recent studies have shown that above the age of 20, the production of Glutathione decreases by 1 percent each year due to toxic overloads, poor diet, and free radical stress.

Scientific studies have explored the impact of meditation on glutathione levels and its potential role in promoting longevity. A well-cited study published in the Journal of Alternative and Complementary Medicine (Sinha et al, 2007) showed that, alongside yoga, meditation boosts this powerhouse peptide by a whopping 41%

A review article published in the journal Antioxidants in 2020 examined the relationship between meditation and oxidative stress. The review highlighted multiple studies that consistently found meditation to be associated with decreased oxidative stress markers and increased antioxidant capacity, including the production of Glutathione.

Furthermore, a study published in the journal Psycho Neuroendocrinology in 2021 investigated the effects of a mindfulness-based stress reduction program on glutathione levels in older adults. The results demonstrated that participants showed a significant increase in glutathione levels after the mindfulness program compared to the control group.

These findings indicate that meditation can potentially enhance glutathione levels, promote antioxidant defenses, and reduce oxidative stress, which contributes to the aging process. By mitigating oxidative damage and supporting cellular health, meditation may positively impact longevity and overall well-being.

4. Meditation reduces cellular Aging and helps us live long:

Moderate consumption of red wine has been associated with potential life extension, and one of the key components responsible for this effect is **resveratrol.** Resveratrol acts as a strong antioxidant and has been found to activate a family of genes and proteins known as "sirtuins," which are associated with longevity.

In a study published in the journal Oxidative Medicine and Cellular Longevity in 2017 (Tolahunase et al.), the impact of meditation on cellular aging was investigated in a group of 96 participants over 12 weeks.

The study revealed that meditation significantly reduced the rate of cellular aging in apparently healthy individuals. The researchers found that meditation substantially increased 52% in Sirtuin 1, a key protein associated with longevity.

These findings suggest that meditation may contribute to cellular rejuvenation and the activation of longevity-associated proteins such as Sirtuin 1. By reducing cellular aging, meditation can promote a longer and healthier lifespan.

5. Look Younger: Meditation Slows Skin Aging, Reduces Wrinkles:

The best anti-aging solution for our skin doesn't come in a bottle or tube. Chronic inflammation is a major contributor to accelerated aging, leading us to look older than our actual age. Stress is recognized as the primary cause of chronic inflammation.

When we experience stress, our body releases cortisol, which can elevate blood sugar levels. The binding of sugar to proteins and lipids through glycation generates advanced glycation end products, releasing reactive oxygen radicals. This leads to oxidative stress, causing a significant reduction in the body's levels of essential antioxidants like glutathione, vitamin C, and vitamin E. Consequently, this can disrupt collagen synthesis in skin tissues, leading to wrinkles, loss of elasticity, and dullness.

Meditation serves as a powerful tool to combat stress and its effects on our skin. By cultivating a regular meditation practice, we become more resilient to stress, which can positively impact our skin health. Meditation has been shown to modulate the activity of proteins such as **NF-κB,** which regulate the skin's aging process.

In 2013, researchers from UCLA (Black et al.) found that after practicing meditation for 8 weeks, protein NF-κB was significantly turned off. Meditation is the fountain of youth for the skin.

Further, a study published in the journal Brain, Behavior, and Immunity in 2020 (Buric et al.) examined the effects of meditation on stress reduction and skin aging in a group of adults. The study found that participants who practiced meditation exhibited lower levels of the stress hormone cortisol and reported improved skin appearance, including reduced wrinkles and improved skin elasticity.

Furthermore, a study published in the journal Psycho neuroendocrinology in 2021 (Epel et al.) investigated the impact of a mindfulness meditation program on cellular aging markers in a group of women. The results demonstrated that after the meditation program, participants showed significant reductions in markers of cellular aging, including reduced activity of genes associated with inflammation and enhanced activity of genes related to cellular repair and maintenance.

These recent scientific findings indicate that meditation can positively affect skin aging. Incorporating meditation into our lifestyle may provide an additional tool for managing stress, reducing inflammation, and promoting healthier skin aging, ultimately contributing to a youthful appearance.

6. Meditation Keeps Dementia and Alzheimer's Away:

Neurotrophic factors are molecules that play a crucial role in enhancing the growth and survival of neurons. Brain-derived neurotrophic **Factor (BDNF)** is particularly important for memory formation, learning, and higher-level cognitive functions that tend to decline as we age. BDNF is often referred to as the "king of all neurotrophins" as it not only supports the development of new neurons and synapses but also repairs and strengthens existing neural circuits, effectively reversing age-related brain cell death through neurogenesis.

Low levels of BDNF have been associated with various age-related brain disorders, including Alzheimer's disease, Parkinson's disease, Huntington's disease, and dementia.

In a study conducted by Professor of Clinical Psychology Rael Cahn M.D. and colleagues at the University of Southern California (USC) in 2017, 38 participants underwent a three-month meditation retreat. The study found that these individuals who practiced meditation experienced a remarkable increase in their BDNF levels. Specifically, their BDNF levels rose by an impressive 280%, from 2513 to 7039 pg/ml.

Recent scientific studies have investigated the relationship between meditation, BDNF, and the prevention of dementia and Alzheimer's disease. A study published in the Journal of Alzheimer's Disease in 2021 (Solé-Padullés et al.) examined the effects of a long-term meditation practice on BDNF levels and cognitive function in a group of older adults.

The results showed that individuals who had engaged in regular meditation for several years had higher BDNF levels compared to non-meditators. Moreover, higher BDNF levels were associated with better cognitive performance, suggesting a potential protective effect against cognitive decline.

These latest scientific findings suggest that meditation may play a role in preventing dementia and Alzheimer's disease by promoting the production of BDNF. By increasing BDNF levels, meditation could enhance neuroplasticity, support neuronal survival, and improve cognitive function. By significantly boosting BDNF levels, meditation acts as a powerful tool in promoting brain health, cognitive function, and overall well-being throughout life. It may help protect against age-related brain degenerative diseases such as dementia and Alzheimer's, allowing individuals to maintain their cognitive abilities and prevent mental decline.

Chapter-4

Meditation Helps: Lose Weight, Achieve Ideal Body

1. Meditation Burns Belly Fat:

Insulin resistance is a significant risk factor for the development of type 2 diabetes and is closely associated with obesity. The excess glucose circulating in the bloodstream of insulin-resistant individuals often gets stored as visceral fat, which is related to several health problems.

Research has shown that chronic stress can lead to insulin resistance by increasing **cortisol levels.** This, in turn, causes excess glucose to accumulate in the bloodstream, which can lead to the development of visceral fat and other health problems.

In a recent study published in the journal Obesity, researchers found that practicing mindfulness meditation can help to reduce visceral fat and improve insulin sensitivity. The study involved 47 overweight or obese adults randomly assigned to mindfulness meditation or a control group. Those in the meditation group practiced for 30 minutes a day, six days a week, for eight weeks. At the end of the study, the mindfulness meditation group significantly reduced their visceral fat levels and improved their insulin sensitivity compared to the control group. This suggests that mindfulness meditation may be an effective way to reduce the risk of developing type 2 diabetes and other health problems associated with insulin resistance.

2. Meditation cures Food addiction and Overeating:

The blood sugar level and dopamine rush we get after wiping out our junk food make us feel on cloud nine, and one has no better feeling in the world for a while, and one is addicted to food and overeating. But for the meditators' **dopamine levels** remained high and tight, day and night without addiction.

A landmark 2002 study at the John F. Kennedy Institute (Kjaer et al) found that dopamine levels were boosted by 65% during meditation.

Some research also suggests that meditation may positively affect hormones related to appetite regulation, such as **leptin and ghrelin**. Leptin is responsible for signaling fullness, while ghrelin stimulates appetite. Meditation may help balance these hormones, potentially reducing excessive hunger and overeating.

3. Meditation Activates our Body's Fat Burning Furnace:

Cortisol is a hormone that is released in response to stress. Chronic stress makes our body think we must get fat for later. Elevated cortisol levels over prolonged periods have been associated with various health issues, including weight gain and increased fat accumulation, especially in the abdominal area. High cortisol levels can also increase appetite and cravings for high-calorie comfort foods.

Meditation has been studied for its potential to reduce stress and lower cortisol levels, thus indirectly influencing fat burning. Cortisol interferes with our sleep, eats away at our muscles, makes us anxious and depressed, sparks widespread tissue inflammation, sandbags our digestive system, and stonewalls our immune system.

In 2013, University of California-Davis (Saron et al.) researchers found that meditation cuts cortisol levels by more than half. For those of us wishing to be lighter on our feet, dramatically reducing our stress hormones relaxes our body, quiets our mind, and cools off our overheated amygdala. Meditation is a panacea for stress.

4. Meditation helps to Gain Power Over our Food:

In a study at Cornell University in 2015 led by Brian Wansink, PhD, researchers delved into the habits of 61 individuals who effortlessly maintained a slim figure. The study aimed to uncover the simple behaviors that played a significant role in their weight management. The key finding was that these individuals were highly attuned to their body's internal signals, such as when, what, and how much to eat. In essence, they were mindful eaters—whether or not they were aware of it.

Mindful eating, which involves eating food with slow, deliberate bites, satisfies the body's pleasure receptors and ensures that nourishment aligns with physical needs. Eating when the body need is far more enjoyable and fulfilling than mindless overeating. The increased mindfulness that comes with this practice encourages individuals to make more conscious food choices, leading them to nutritious, whole foods that nourish the body rather than unhealthy or highly processed options.

Research has shown that mindful eaters lose weight 633% more effectively than those who don't practice mindfulness. By incorporating meditation into daily routine, one can cultivate this cautious approach to eating, empowering to make healthier food choices and developing a positive relationship with nourishment. The combination of mindfulness and meditation not only leads to a healthier, more balanced lifestyle but fosters a deeper connection with the body's needs.

5. Meditation Activates our body's Relaxation Response:

Instead of feeling our uncomfortable emotions, we turn to food. It does nothing to address our emotional issues on other hand make matter worse. Meditation helps in activating our body's "relaxation response." Term Coined by the esteemed Harvard cardiologist Dr. Herbert Benson in the 1980s, this is "opposite of stress" response.

When the body is in a state of stress, various physiological changes occur, such as increased heart rate, breathing , blood pressure, and also the release of stress hormones such as cortisol and adrenaline. The relaxation response, on the other hand, promotes a state of calm and healing, allowing the body to rest and recuperate. Meditation triggers a relaxation response by activating the parasympathetic nervous system. Meditation help us to be aware of the present moment by reducing the 60,000 thoughts the human mind thinks daily.

By regularly practicing meditation, individuals can strengthen their ability to elicit a relaxation response, promoting a state of calm, healing, and restoration for the body and mind. This can lead to numerous health benefits, including reduced stress, improved immune function, better sleep, and enhanced well-being.

Chapter-5

Meditation, Naturally Boosts Good Brain Chemicals

1. Meditation Boosts Endorphins- The internal Painkiller:

Endorphins are the body's neurotransmitters, known for their pain-relieving and mood-enhancing properties. They are often referred to as "feel-good" chemicals as they can create a sense of euphoria and reduce sensations of pain. Some research suggests that Meditation can influence the brain's opioid receptors, which are the same receptors targeted by externally administered painkillers.

Activation of these receptors can trigger the release of endorphins.

A study (Harte et al.) published in the Biological Psychology Journal in 1995 post-tested the neurochemical release of two groups: 11 elite runners and 12 highly trained meditators. The researchers concluded that Meditation's "feel-good effect" scored even higher than running.

2. Meditation Boosts GABA- The Calm Chemical:

Best known for making us feel calm, GABA (gamma amino butyric acid) is one of the major inhibitory neurotransmitters in our central nervous system that plays a crucial role in regulating brain activity. It is an inhibitory neurotransmitter that helps reduce neuronal activity and has a calming effect on the brain. GABA is involved in various functions, including anxiety regulation, stress management, sleep promotion, and overall emotional balance. Meditation has been found to boost GABA levels in the brain, increasing calmness and relaxation.

Anyone with an addiction, including alcohol, drugs, caffeine, and food, have one thing in common and that is the lack of GABA. Not having enough GABA can create many problems, including anxiety, nervousness, racing thoughts, and sleeplessness.

In 2010 in a study at Boston University, found a 27% increase in GABA levels after 60 minutes of meditation.

3. Meditation Boosts Serotonin- The Happy Neurotransmitter:

Most of the approximately 86 billion brain cells are influenced by serotonin. Serotonin is often referred to as the "happy neurotransmitter" because it plays a vital role in regulating mood, emotions, and overall well-being. It is also involved in various physiological processes, including sleep, appetite, and pain perception.

Serotonin is key to helping relay signals from one part of the brain to another. This crucial chemical has a profound impact on our mood and contributes greatly to our overall state of well-being.

According to Princeton brain researcher Barry Jacobs, Ph.D., depression sets in when fewer and fewer new brain cells are created, with stress and age being the leading trigger. The University of Montreal scientists (Perreau-Linck et al) have shown that activities like mindfulness directly impact the brain's serotonin levels. It is thought that meditation " help neurons bathe with an array of feel-good chemical, melting away the stress that leads to low level of serotonin.

Meditation boosts serotonin levels and supports emotional well-being. Its serotonin-replenishing effect creates a utopian chemical environment for producing new brain cells, making people happier and healthier.

4. Meditation Boosts DHEA- The Longevity Molecule:

DHEA (De hydro epiandrosterone) is a hormone produced by the adrenal glands, it serves as a precursor to other hormones, including estrogen and testosterone. DHEA plays a role in various physiological processes, such as immune function, metabolism, and stress response.

Also known as the "longevity molecule" DHEA is one of the most important hormones in the body. As we age, our DHEA levels decrease yearly, cusing accelrated aging and diseases.

Doctors have measured DHEA levels to find a patient's physiological "true age", a far more accurate health marker than "age in years." In fact, a 12 year study of 240 men (50-79 years) found that DHEA levels were directly linked to mortality. The researchers' findings were simple yet impactful: the less DHEA you have, the fewer years you have left.

Luckily, meditation provides a dramatic boost in DHEA hormone levels. Dr. Vincent Giampapa, M.D., former President of the American Board of Anti-Aging Medicine and current prominent longevity researcher, discovered that meditation practitioners have an incredible 43.77% more DHEA than everybody else.

5. Meditation Boosts Melatonin- The Sleep Molecule:

Melatonin is referred as "the sleep molecule." It is produced by the pineal gland in the brain. Melatonin plays a crucial role in regulating the sleep-wake cycle (circadian rhythm). Melatonin levels typically rise in the evening, signaling the body that it is time to prepare for sleep, and decrease in the morning, signaling wakefulness.

A "Superhero", melatonin is known to prevent cancer, strengthen the immune system, slow down aging, and has also been linked to helping prevent over 100 different diseases.

Excessive light is the number "1" enemy of melatonin, shutting down our body's production of this chemical. Luckily, there is an efficient, solution. Rutgers University researchers discovered that melatonin levels for meditation practitioners were boosted by an average of 98%, with many participants having more than an incredible 300% increase.

6. Meditation Boosts Growth Hormone- Fountain of Youth:

Growth hormone (GH), or somatotropin, is produced by the pituitary gland at the base of the brain. GH plays a crucial role in various physiological processes, growth and development during childhood and adolescence. However, GH remains essential for maintaining healthy body composition, metabolism, and tissue repair throughout life. Various factors, including the sleep-wake cycle, stress, exercise, and nutrition, regulate growth hormone secretion. Its secretion is pulsatile, meaning it occurs in bursts throughout the day, with the most significant bursts typically happening during deep sleep, especially during the early hours of the night.

GH stimulates growth during childhood. Starting in the 40s, your pituitary gland, at the base of brain where growth hormone is produced, gradually decreases the amount of GH it creates. The body's diminishing supply of growth hormone causes the frailty that comes with aging—weaker bones and muscles, increased body fat, poor heart contractions, lack of motivation, and fatigue.

Our body release most growth hormone, in "Delta," state A brainwave frequency which is dominant during both meditation and deep sleep. Are meditators' naturally elevated growth hormone levels why they tend to look so young and healthy? Scientists think so. Meditation effectively turns back the clock.

7. Meditation reduces Cortisol- The Stress Hormones:

Cortisol is a major age-accelerating hormone that the body releases in response to stress and plays a critical role in the fight-or-flight response. However, chronic or prolonged stress can lead to consistently elevated cortisol levels, which may have negative effects on health and well-being. Cortisol is the one chemical where less is better. When we are stressed, our bodies produce cortisol and adrenaline in abundance.

Research suggests that regular meditation practice helps reduce cortisol levels. When individuals engage in meditation, they enter a state of relaxation, which triggers the body's relaxation response. This response, in turn, reduces the production of stress hormones like cortisol. Chronic stress can lead to an overproduction of cortisol, which can have adverse effects on the body and mind, including anxiety, sleep disturbances, and impaired cognitive function.

By engaging in meditation regularly, individuals can experience a decrease in stress levels, which, in turn, helps regulate cortisol production and mitigate the negative effects of chronic stress.

CHAPTER-6

Meditation: Boost Immunity, Build Health, Beat Disease.

1. Meditation Fortify Our Health Front line immunity warriors:

The immune system is critical in defending the body against infections and diseases.

According to scientists, each of us has a bulletproof defense system consisting of antibodies and antigens. Antibodies' job is to correctly identify invaders (called antigens) such as viruses, bacteria, and germs. After finding out precisely "who" is invading, antibodies will attach themselves to the offenders (antigens), effectively "marking them for death."

T cells (also called T lymphocytes) are one of the significant components of the adaptive immune system. Their roles include:

- Directly killing infected host cells.
- Activating other immune cells.
- Producing cytokines.

- Regulating the immune response.

Some studies have suggested that meditation and mindfulness positively affect the immune system. One hypothesis is that reducing stress through meditation may lead to lower levels of stress hormones like cortisol, which, in turn, could positively impact immune function. Additionally, meditation may promote overall well-being and healthy lifestyle behaviors, contributing to improved immune health.

An 8-week UCLA study found that, for 50 HIV-positive men, only 30-45 minutes of mindfulness meditation per day stopped the decline of T cells, and even halted the progression of disease.

2. Meditation keep our Gene Cells and DNA Healthy:

Our body is made up of trillions of cells these cells. When our cells work together in harmony, we are healthy. Dr. Bruce Lipton, a biologist at Stanford, discovered that the cell's "brain" isn't in the nucleus but in its protective membrane. Our beliefs, emotions, and experiences influence this membrane's actions. So, by mastering our thoughts through meditation, we can improve our cell health.

In his book *The Biology of Belief*, Dr. Lipton explains that since our mind controls our cells, genes, and DNA, we can "think our way to excellent health." Our approach to health has changed, and meditation is key to controlling it.

3. Meditation Activate Self-Healing Power of Our Body:

Psychoneuroimmunology (PNI) explores the connection between our brain and the immune system. Did you know that we can produce cancer-fighting chemicals worth millions of dollars by retraining our brains?

One of these chemicals is "Interleukin-2," a powerful drug that stimulates cancer-fighting molecules in the body. What triggers these molecules? Endorphins—those feel-good chemicals released when we're happy.

Dr. Deepak Chopra, a world-renowned doctor and author, says that through meditation, we can boost endorphins and create millions of dollars' worth of cancer-fighting Interleukin-2. It's all about the power of the mind and medition is the tool.

4. Meditation has the power to Influence Gene Expression:

A person's genes are not just controlled by their DNA sequence—they're also influenced by factors like nutrition, behavior, and stress. Stress, for example, can cause changes in the brain's DNA that might lead to neurological problems. In other words, we are shaped by what we eat, drink, and how active we are. We don't have to rely on our parents' genetics to determine our health—we can change it through our thoughts and actions.

Meditation is one powerful way to change our genetic blueprint. It helps us break free from being victims of our inherited DNA. Dr. Dean Ornish and his team at the University of California, San Francisco, found that meditation can even "silence" the genes linked to cancer. In their study, prostate cancer survivors who practiced meditative breathing reduced the expression of cancer-associated genes, showing that meditation can actually help prevent disease at the molecular level.

5. Meditation down-regulate Modern Epidemic Inflammation:

Inflammation is a major health problem today, linked to many diseases. Chronic inflammation is a toxic condition, especially harmful to the brain. It is connected to a wide range of health issues, from anxiety and addiction to arthritis, cancer, depression, heart disease, and obesity.

A recent study shows that meditation can help fight inflammation. After just 8 hours of practice, meditation "down-regulated" key genes related to inflammation, like RIPK2, COX2, and HDAC, which are also targeted by anti-inflammatory drugs.

According to Richard J. Davidson, a professor at UW–Madison, this research shows that the calmness of our mind can influence how our genes express themselves. Meditation acts like a powerful firefighting team, helping to control the body's internal "wildfires" that lead to disease. All it takes is the willingness to try.

6. Meditation influences our Gut- Gut-Brain Axis:

Chronic inflammation is a growing health issue today, and it's linked to many diseases, such as anxiety, addiction, arthritis, asthma, cancer, depression, heart disease, and obesity. This ongoing inflammation, especially in the brain, harms the body and can worsen conditions over time.

A recent study shows that meditation can help reduce inflammation. After just 8 hours of practice, meditation helped lower the activity of several key genes involved in inflammation, which are also targeted by anti-inflammatory medications.

Richard J. Davidson, a professor at the University of Wisconsin, explained that this research shows how the calmness we achieve through meditation can affect how our genes work. In essence, meditation acts like a powerful tool to reduce inflammation and fight diseases linked to it. All it takes is practicing meditation to activate these benefits. With this we conclude this part of book on benefits of meditation.

I request you to understand all these benefits well, do your own researches and find some reasons to motivate you to do meditation.

Understanding these benefits also shed light on why meditation is gaining global popularity and why it is widely regarded as the best tool for stress management and mental wellbeing.

I hope no one would want to miss out on these benefits.

I also hope that by observing the positive effects of meditation, many of you will be inspired to learn more about it and incorporate it into your daily lives.

Part V:
Meditation Practice

CHATER-1

Meditation Practice

Welcome to the discussion on the last part of this book, which is Meditation practice.

In order to reap the benefits of meditation, it is very important to practice meditation in the beginning until it becomes part of life and happens naturally, requiring no effort.

It is said that the good news about meditation is that we need not practice it, and the bad news is that, as beginners, we have to practice it.

It's difficult to become aware of the inner world and inner thought processes when we are involved in our day-to-day work and dealing with the people around us.

So, in the beginning, we need to find time, find a place where we can sit, and slowly observe ourselves. Observation needs to start from the periphery, from the surroundings, then to the body, then to breath, then to thoughts and emotions.

We can understand the practice of meditation by analogy with riding a bicycle. When we first learn to ride a bicycle, it requires effort and attention.

Initially, to find balance, we keep our backs straight and focus on the road ahead, avoiding distractions to the left or right. We pedal to move forward, but often, we struggle and may fall to one side or the other. It takes time and consistent practice.

Then, one day, we realize we can cycle and maintain balance even if our posture is imperfect or our vision is not straight. We become experts, but this transformation only happens over time.

It demands continuous practice. Just reading about cycle and cycling does not work.

The same principle applies to meditation.

At the outset, we sit with an upright posture to conserve energy and remain attentive.

We try to keep our gaze fixed on the tip of our nostrils to avoid mind movement. However, just like a bicycle swaying left and right, our Mind frequently drifts to thoughts of the past or future.

To stay in the present and avoid wandering, we maintain continuous observation, focusing on our breath or the sensation happening in the present. With regular practice, we can train our Minds to stay in the present and observe our chosen point of focus.

Currently, our Minds are habituated to running and thinking continuously. That is how we have been trained in schools and colleges, but no training is imparted to make Mind salient and calm.

Our minds have become habitual wanderers. Now, our Minds are beyond our control. They have become masters and are not listening to us. Meditation is our effort to bring the Mind home and master it.

Through regular meditation practice, a time will come when there is no need to force or sit down with effort; meditation happens naturally; it's like becoming so proficient at riding a bicycle that it feels effortless.

To progress in meditation, the Mind is purified through Yama and Niyama, and the body is purified through Asanas and Pranayamas, as suggested by Sage Patanjali in the Yoga Sutra. Body and Mind must be purified simultaneously, as a healthy mind lives in a healthy body.

Asanas are the physio psychological postures, help us to relive all strain, and stress we have accumulated in this body, it prepares us for meditation.

During asana, we watch the body and the unconscious Mind. During pranayama, we watch the breath. Finally, we create a possibility to watch the thought in meditation.

So, the practice of asanas and pranayama is preparatory for meditation. It eases our journey, makes our systems healthy, improves our flexibility, and makes us relax. A relaxed body dwells only a calm and peaceful mind.

We live in this body our whole lives; it's our permanent residence. Why not make it a place worth living in?

With regular practice, we start having clarity of thought, our willpower increases, which eases our journey.

Based on my experience and understanding, I have devised some guided meditations based on the learning of pratyahara/ dharna and Dhyana, or the learning of contemplation, concentration, and meditation discussed in this book.

I am sharing a script for meditation. You can record the same in your voice or remember the sequence and practice it. You can easily understand the concept if you go through the script without any recorded voice. Three scripts for guided meditations are shared: one for pratyahara, i.e., contemplation-; one for pratyahara and dharna- together, i.e., contemplation and concentration; and the third and final one with pratyahara/ dharna and Dhyana. i.e., contemplation, concentration, and meditation; each session lasts about 12-15 minutes.

To make meditation a part of daily life, I recommend finding a fixed place and fixed time daily and anchoring your practice with some daily habits.

For progress in meditation, it is recommended that you first do guided meditation, session one, for 21 days, then guided meditation, session two, for 21 days, and after that start guided meditation session three and continue to practice it. You can even do it for 25 to 30 minutes.

Later, you can devise your own ways of meditation or not require any method.

With this, we conclude our session on meditation practice.

We have also come to the end of this book and will conclude it.

It's been an incredible journey.

I hope this book will inspire you to make meditation a part of your life. Now you must know what IS MEDITATION, why WE DO MEDITATION, and HOW TO DO MEDITATION. If we don't practice, then all knowledge is of no value. One ounce of experience is more than tons of knowledge, so don't forget to practice to reap the numerous benefits of meditation.

Meditation is a journey inwards; everyone has to pave his way, crossing the hurdles with his understanding and traveling alone. As we explore ourselves and experience, we get to know meditation better.

I thank you for showing interest in learning meditation and congratulate you on completing this book. I hope the knowledge gained through this book will continue to inspire and guide you. If you found this book helpful, kindly recommend it to your friends, relatives, and colleagues.

Further, I am open to any opportunity to collaborate with government organizations or civil societies/unions/NGOs that would allow me to serve the broader community.

Finally, I wish you all a prosperous, peaceful, stress-free, and JOYFUL MEDITATIVE life.

With this, Goodbye from my end.

Best of luck on your meditation journey.

Thank you, one and all.

Contact at-   yogajourney2@gmail.com

Guided Meditation:1
Practice of Contemplation

ALL FIVE SENSE

Hello, welcome to the guided mediation.

You can sit on the floor or a chair.

Before we start prepare yourself

Move your body left and right, forward and backward.

Adjust your self and Sit in a comfortable posture.

Once you are ready,

Place your palms on your lap, facing upward, you can interlock your fingers as well.

Keep your spine, neck, and head in a straight line; you can take support on back.

Now gently close your eyes.

Take a deep breath,

and exhale completely.

Keep breathing deeply and slowly.

Now we will become aware of five senses and move inward.

Shift your focus to grossest of all sense. i.e. sense of hearing.

Simply hear, all sounds coming from far. It may sound of vehicle, people talking

Hear what you are hearing, do not judge.

Now bring your focus to sounds coming from nearby or room you are sitting.

It may be sound of fan or ticking of clock

Just hear do not interpret.

Now focus more, and try to hear the sound your body is making. The sound of your heart beat, the sound of your breath.

Hear what you are hearing.

If you mind goes here and there, gently guide it back to the sense of hearing.

Now move your attention from sense of hearing to sense of touch

Feel the touch of your body on the floor or the chair.

Take awareness to your both leg and feel, it may be sensation of pain, discomfort or itching.

Now feel your lower, middle and upper back and shoulder and become aware of all sensation.

Let sensation come and go, do not jude, No liking or disliking.

Shift awareness to your trunk, hands, neck, face and head, feel what you are feeling right now.

Now Scan whole body and feel whatever you are feeling.

If you find your mind wandering, gently guide it back to the bodily sensations and the present moment.

Now move your awareness from sense of touch to the sense of vision.

Fix your eye balls on tip of nostril.

See what you are seeing right now, it may be the darkness or the some light.

Do not move your eye ball.

If mind goes here and there bring it back and keep focusing on tip of nostril.

Experience that mind is calming down

Now from sense of vision move to sense of taste.

Become fully aware of sense of taste and taste what you tasting right now.

If there is no taste become aware of taste of no taste.

Taste what you taste right now

If mind goes here and there bring it back and keep focusing on sensation of taste.

Now from sense of taste, move to the most subtlest of sensation, sense of smell. With inhalation, smell

It may be fragrance of room freshener or smell of your perfume or your body odor

Smell what you smell

If mind wonders bring it back to sense of smell.

We have Waken up all the five sense and moved inward.

Now engage senses together, hear all sound and same time feel touch of your body on floor or chair, and also become aware of darkness at tip of nostril and sense if any smell is there.

Be in this present moment using your sense and go inward.

If mind goes here and there bring it back to this moment engaging with senses.

Become aware your breath is slow and deep, and your mind is calm and peaceful.

Experience, feel this moment. Allow this feeling to deepen with each practice.

Take a deep breath; we will come out of meditative state,

Feel your breath, Feel your whole body. Become aware of your surroundings.

We will now conclude the session.

Adopt namaskar mudra.

Bow down to Mother Earth and express your gratitude take blessings of mother earth.

Gently come up, Rub your palms together, make cup of your palm, cover your eyes, and open your eyes inside. Gently massage your face and Release your palms.

Thank you for participating in this meditation.

Keep meditating.

Guided Meditation:2
Practice of Contemplation
and Concentrations

FIVE SENS AND BREATH

Hello, welcome to the guided mediation.

You can sit on the floor or a chair.

Before we start prepare yourself

Move your body left and right, forward and backward.

Adjust your self and Sit in a comfortable posture.

Once you are ready,

Place your palms on your lap, facing upward, you can interlock your fingers as well.

Keep your spine, neck, and head in a straight line; you can take support on back.

Now gently close your eyes.

Take a deep breath,

and exhale completely.

Keep breathing deeply and slowly.

We will quickly become aware of five senses and move inward.

Simply hear, all sounds coming far.

Focus on nearby sounds.

Now try to hear the sound of your breath.

From sound Move to sense of touch and scan your whole body

Feel what you are feeling.

Take a deep breath , go deeper fix your both eye ball on tip of nostril and do not allow your eye ball to move.

Now become aware of sense of taste and Taste what you tasting, right now.

Take deep breath and

deeper and while inhalation Smell what you're smelling.

Now engage senses, together and bring your whole focus to your breath,

Try to hear the sound of incoming air at the entrance of nostril

Feel the air touching at the entrance of nostril above upper lips

Fix your gaze at entrance of nostril try to see the incoming air

Try to Smell it , at the entrance of nostril

Engage all your sense on breath

Keep observing incoming and outgoing breath using all the senses

If mind goes here and there bring it back to this moment engaging with senses, focusing on breath.

Keep observing the breath, as it goes in and out.

feel Stay present and focused.

Now, let's deepen our awareness of the breath.

Feel the passage of breath through your nostrils, nasal passages, throat, windpipe, bronchi, and into the lungs.

Notice your belly rising with each incoming breath and falling with each outgoing breath.

Feel the passage of the outgoing breath as well

Let your awareness move in and out with the breath.

Follow the breath inward as it goes in and follow the outward as it comes out.

If your mind wanders, gently bring it back to the breath and continue observing.

Keep observing the breath

Now become more aware and, Feel the breath going in and observe the gap of no breath before the breath comes out.

Observe the outgoing breath and the gap of no breath before inhalation.

BREATH GOES IN IT STOPS, we exhale   BREATH GOES OUT, and IT STOPOS

Focus on these gaps and be aware of the natural pause of breath.

Inhale breath goes in, before we exhale it stops

We exhale breath comes out, before we inhale it stops.

Be in those two gaps.

If your mind wanders, gently bring it back to the breath and continue observing the gap of no breath.

Don't manipulate it, just watch and observe.

The breath goes in, it stops, the breath comes out it stops....

Observe the duration of gap is increasing and you are able to see those gaps.

If your mind wanders, it goes here and there , bring it back to the breath and keep watching.

The gaps are refreshing and rejuvenating,

Stay alert and awake

Become aware your breath is slow and deep, and your mind is calm and peaceful.

Feel this moment. Allow this feeling to deepen with each practice.

Take a breath; we will come out of meditative state,

Feel your breath, Feel your whole body. SCAN IT from toes to head. Become aware of your surroundings.

We will now conclude the session.

Adopt namaskar mudra.

Bow down to Mother Earth and express gratitude , take blessings of mother earth.

Gently come up, Rub your palms together, make cup of your palm, cover your eyes, and open your eyes inside. Gently massage your face and Release your palms.

Thank you for participating in this meditation.

Keep meditating.

Guided Meditation-3
Practice of Contemplation, concentration and Meditation.

FIVE SENS AND BREATH AND MIND

Hello, welcome to the guided mediation.

You can sit on the floor or a chair.

Before we start prepare yourself

Move your body left and right, forward and backward.

Adjust your self and Sit in a comfortable posture.

Once you are ready,

Place your palms on your lap, facing upward, you can interlock your fingers as well.

Keep your spine, neck, and head in a straight line; you can take support on back.

Now gently close your eyes.

Take a deep breath,

and exhale completely.

Keep breathing deeply and slowly.

We will become aware of five senses and move inward.

Hear what you are hearing

Come to your body and Feel what you are feeling right

Fix your gaze on tip of nostril and see what you are seeing

Go deeper and taste what you tasting right now

Take a deep breath and smell what you smelling now

Now engage all senses together and bring your whole focus to your breath, at the entrance of nostril

Try to hear the sound of incoming air

Feel the air touching at the entrance of nostril

Fix your gaze at entrance of nostril try to see the incoming air

Try to Smell incoming air at the entrance nostril

Engage all your sense on breath

Keep observing incoming and outgoing breath.

If mind goes here and there bring it back to this moment, engaging with senses, focusing on breath.

Now

Feel the passage of breath through your nostrils, nasal passages, throat, windpipe, bronchi, and into the lungs.

Notice your belly rising with each incoming breath and falling with each outgoing breath.

Feel the passage of the outgoing breath

If mind wonders bring it back to observing the breath

Now become more aware and , Feel the breath going in and observe the gap of no breath before the breath comes out.

Observe the breath coming out h and the gap of no breath before the next inhalation.

BREATH GOES IN IT STOPS   BREATH GOES OUT IT STOPOS

Focus on these gaps and be aware of the natural pause of bre

Now, let's shift our attention on observing the thoughts. Ask yourself, what is the next thought in my mind?

keep observing.

If thought come, Don't suppress, just watch without any judgment.

Again ask your self what is the next thought in my mind

Watch thoughts without any judgment

See from where these thoughts coming—whether it's the from the head, tongue, throat, heart, or naval center.

Be aware and just watch.

Maintain your distance from thoughts. remain unidentified

When thoughts arise, be indifferent and don't give them any energy.

Keep observing the thoughts

When thought arises ignore them, treat them as uninvited guests

Again Ask yourself, "What is the next thought?" This question brings awareness, and in that awareness, the process of thinking comes to a halt.

Experience this stillness, silence, and peacefulness.

Keep watching thoughts

If any thoughts arise, don't feel bad about them.

Let them come and go like clouds .

Keep watching the thoughts.

Keep watching the mind.

Keep observing the thoughts

Become aware your breath has become slower , deeper, and mind is calm and peaceful.

We are witnessing ourselves.

Experience, feel this moment. Allow this feeling to deepen with each practice.

Take a breath; we will come out of meditative state,

Feel your breath, Feel your whole body. Become aware of your surroundings.

We will now conclude the session.

Adopt the namaskar mudra.

Bow down to Mother Earth and express gratitude take blessings of mother earth.

Gently come up, Rub your palms together, make cup of your palm, cover your eyes, and open your eyes inside. Gently massage your face and Release your palms.

Thank you for participating in this meditation.

Keep meditating.

Bibliography: Resources

1. Patajali Yoga Sutra- by Swami Vivekananda, Published by Fingerprint Publishing

2. "Autobiography of a Yogi" by Paramahansa Yogananda, Published by Yogoda Satsanga Society of India

3. "The Heart of Yoga: Developing a Personal Practice" by T.K.V. Desikachar, Published by Inner Traditions.

4. Total Meditation by Deepak Chopra, MD. Published by Harmony

5. Swami Vivekananda "The Complete Works of Swami Vivekananda", Vol 1 to IX, Pub. Advaita Ashram.

6. The Light on Yoga by BKS Iyenger, Published by Thorsons

7. Yoga, Moving to the Centre, by Osho, Fusion Books.

8. 112 Meditations for Self Realization by Ranjit Chaudhri, Published by Fingerprint Publishing.

9. What is Meditation by J Krishnamurthy, Publisher Rider & Co

10. The Art of Living: Vipassana Meditation, by William Hart, Published by Vipassana Research Institute

11. Indian Philosophy, Vol 1 and Vol 2 by S Radhakrishnan, Publisher Oxford.

12. Monitoring Editor: Alexander Muacevic and John R Adler Meditation and Its Mental and

    Physical Health Benefits in 2023 [PMC free article] [PubMed] [Google Scholar]

13. Asana Pranayama Mudra Bandha, by Swami Satyananda, Swami Saraswati, Published by Yoga Publication Trust.

14. First and last Freedom: J Krishnamurthy, Publisher Rider & Co

www.ingramcontent.com/pod-product-compliance
Lightning Source LLC
LaVergne TN
LVHW041606070526
838199LV00052B/3008